ARTIFICIAL IN' TRANSHUMANISM & THE DE-EVOLUTION OF DEMOCRACY

Global Chaos
The Precursor to the One-World Dictator

Richard R. Schmidt, D.Min, Ph.D.
Foreword: Jim Schneider
Executive Director VCY America

www.ProphecyFocusMinistries.com

Scripture taken from the New King James Version. Copyright © 1982 by Thomas Nelson, Inc. Used by permission. All rights reserved.

Editor in Chief: Mary Rebholtz
Cover Design By: Valori L. Schmidt

ARTIFICIAL INTELLIGENCE (AI) & THE DE-EVOLUTION OF DEMOCRACY - DECISION 2024
Global Chaos - The Precursor to the One-World Dictator

ISBN-13: 9798859051588

P.O. Box 122
Hales, Corners, WI 53130
www.ProphecyFocusMinistries.com

All rights reserved. No part of this publication may be reproduced, stored in a retrieval system, or transmitted in any form or by any means—electronic, mechanical, digital, photocopy, recording, or any other—except for brief quotations in printed reviews, without the prior permission of the publisher. All internet sites that have cooperative share agreements for their content is also agreed to for reproduction and use of this content.

Prophecy Focus Ministries, Inc. is recognized by the Internal Revenue Service as a **501(c)(3)** corporation. This book is designed to advance transformational research in Biblical/theological education.

Printed in the **United States of America**

CONTENTS

ACKNOWLEDGEMENTS VII
FOREWORD... XI
   Jim Schneder, Executive Director, VCY America................ XI
PREFACE.. XIII
CHAPTER ONE... 3
   Artificial Intelligence (AI) Defined.. 3
      Artificial Intelligence Ten Developmental Levels............... 3
         Introduction to the Ten Levels of Artificial Intelligence. 3
      Present Levels of Artificial Intelligence............................ 3
         Level One - One-Rule Artificial Intelligence..................... 3
         Level Two – Context Based Artificial Intelligence............ 4
         Level Three - Narrow Domain Artificial Intelligence........ 5
         Level Four - Rational Artificial Intelligence...................... 6
      Predicted Levels of Artificial Intelligence........................... 10
         Level Five – Self-Aware Artificial Intelligence................. 10
         Level Six - Artificial General Intelligence (AGI)................ 12
         Level Seven - Artificial Super Intelligence (ASI).............. 13
         Level Eight - Transcendent AI.. 14
         Level Nine - Cosmic AI... 15
         Level Ten - Godlike AI.. 15
CHAPTER TWO... 19
   Artificial Intelligence (AI) Guaranteed Deception................. 19
   Artificial Intelligence (AI) Deep Faking................................. 23
CHAPTER THREE   41
   Artificial Intelligence (AI) Serious Concerns......................... 41
      Some AI systems perform tasks not trained..................... 42
      We will not notice AI becoming sentient.......................... 42
      Large AI systems are not made of explicit ideas............. 44
      Many AI experts are issuing dire warnings...................... 45
      AI will not care for us... 49
      To survive you have to learn and adapt........................... 51
      Artificial intelligence will soon replace you...................... 52
      AI models and large-scale disinformation........................ 54
      AI is more advanced than realized.................................... 55
   Artificial Intelligence (AI) Ethical Concerns........................... 55
      The Annihilation of Humanity.. 59
      AI Has No Choice But To Kill Us... 63
      Bad Actors of AI.. 64

AI's Existential Risks to Humanity	65
AI's Dependency A Sign of Devastation	67
Alignment of AI with Human Values	68
CHAPTER FOUR	**71**
Transhumanism	71
Introduction to Transhumanism	71
Transhumanism-Advanced Prosthetic Devices	77
Transhumanism-Supernatural Sensory Perception	80
Transhumanism and Artificial General Intelligence	82
Transhumanism and Ethics	85
CHAPTER FIVE	**93**
Transhumanism and Developer's Vision	93
Transhumanism and Superhuman Capabilities	93
Transhumanism and Telepathic Communication	94
Transhumanism and Neural Implants	95
Transhumanism and the Elimination of Disabilities	98
Transhumanism and Colonizing Other Planets	99
Transhumanism and Resurrecting the Dead	100
Transhumanism and Regenerative Medicine	103
Transhumanism and Creativity	106
Transhumanism and Cybercrime	107
Concluding Remarks	109
CHAPTER SIX	**113**
De-Evolution of Democracy	113
Democracy Defined	115
Dictatorship	122
The Descriptive Origin of the Antichrist	123
The Dominant Arrival of the Antichrist	125
The Detestable Character of the Antichrist	128
The Devil's Empowerment of the Antichrist	129
The Deadly Consequences of Rejecting the Antichrist	130
The Destruction of the Antichrist	131
CHAPTER SEVEN	**135**
God's Prophetic Timeline	135
The Satanic Kingdom	136
Two Godly Kingdoms	138
The Universal Kingdom	138
The Theocratic Kingdom	140
Prophecies of the Messianic Kingdom	140
Presentation of the Messianic Kingdom	142

Postponement of the Messianic Kingdom	144
Precursors of the Messianic Kingdom	145
The Mystery Church Revealed	145
The Mystery Church Raptured	146
The Mandatory Seven-Year Tribulation	147
Positive Guarantee of the Messianic Kingdom	151
Abrahamic Covenant	152
Davidic Covenant	152
Land Covenant	153
New Covenant	153
Inauguration of the Messianic Kingdom	154
The Participants in the Messianic Kingdom	155
The Powerful Theocratic Ruler	155
The Productive and Peaceful Environment	156
The Practice of Worship	157
Theological Challenges	158
Covenant Theology	158
Progressive Dispensationalism	160
Conclusion	160
APPENDIX A	163
ChatGPT's Top 84 uses of Artificial Intelligence (AI)	
APPENDIX B	167
ChatGPT Top 100 concepts regarding artificial intelligence	
APPENDIX C	171
ChatGPT Describe in detail how Siri works	
APPENDIX D	173
President Biden's Speech November 2, 2020	
BIBLIOGRAPHY	179

ACKNOWLEDGEMENTS

God placed an incredible group of people in my life whom He has used to not only bring me to saving faith in the Lord Jesus Christ but also to develop my understanding of His most precious Word. When I was in high school, my oldest sister, Kathy (Schmidt) Papala, invited me to a home Bible study, where I heard the gospel for the first time. A few weeks later, I accepted God's free gift of salvation and gave my life to the Lord Jesus Christ.

My wonderful parents, Robert and Charlotte Schmidt, poured their lives into me and encouraged me to love and serve the Lord. My parents are now enjoying heaven's wonders because both accepted the Lord Jesus' gift of salvation in their teen years.

The list of my mentors includes many pastors, Bible college and seminary professors, godly Christians, authors, and theologians. Dr. Sam Horn, who was my pastor for several years while serving in the Milwaukeeland area, encouraged me to start Prophecy Focus Ministries, traveling both nationally and internationally, teaching the prophetic Scriptures. Valori, my precious and talented wife, and I began doing just that. Years later, Dr. Jimmy DeYoung encouraged me to commit my life to recording messages and writing books on the prophetic Word. He was a wonderful mentor, teacher, and encouragement in my ministry. I love him dearly from afar, as he is now home in heaven with his Savior, Jesus Christ. His wife Judy, and their adult children, Rick, Jody, and my very special friend Jimmy Jr., have had a great influence on our ministry, and I love these precious servants of God.

Dr. Les Lofquist, Dr. Henry Vosburgh, and Pastor Chris Allen helped us get started with our first prophecy conferences. These men genuinely embrace helping others for the sake of the gospel. I love these men and thank God for their ministries.

Six years ago, Valori and I made our first trip to the Pre-Tribulation Research Conference in Dallas, Texas, at the suggestion of Mary and Bernie Hertel. Mary and Bernie are two of God's choice servants who pour their lives into studying God's Word and encouraging people in ministry. Their suggestion to go to the Pre-Trib conference was right on target. Many of the men presenting at that conference were individuals whose many books I had read, which provided scholarly insights into the prophetic Scriptures.

Dr. Thomas Ice, Dr. Tim LaHaye, Dr. Ed Hindson, Dr. Randall Price, Dr. Arnold Fruchtenbaum, Dr. Mark Hitchcock, Dr. Andrew Woods, Dr. Michael Rydelnik, and others were there in person at the Pre-Trib conference, and every last one of them was approachable, friendly, and supportive. I genuinely love these men and thank God for their willingness to share their wealth of knowledge with others.

My special thanks to Dr. Thomas Ice and his wonderful wife Janice. I was awestruck by this fine couple, but they treated me as a friend from the first moment we met. In my humble opinion, Dr. Ice is currently the most influential person in defending the pretribulation and premillennial interpretation of Scripture. His website, pre-trib.org, contains many scholarly articles written by excellent theologians. The books he authored are some of the best available on eschatology. I highly encourage everyone not only to get and study his books and read his phenomenal articles, but to support his ministry in prayer and financially.

Several years ago, I attended a Prophecy Up Close conference in Milwaukee, sponsored by the Friends of Israel (FOI) Gospel Ministry. David Levy was one of the speakers, and we immediately started a friendship. That morphed into me flying to New Jersey to meet the FOI director, Jim Showers, and the North American ministries director, Steve Herzig. I had read many of the Friends of Israel published theological books and Bible study commentaries. These men, and many others in the organization, had a very positive impact on my life. I loved traveling to Israel with FOI on their excellent tours, to study the land of the Bible.

Dr. Randall Price and his wonderful wife, Beverly, are another couple that means the world to Valori and me. This couple serves the Lord day and night, and they have been a tremendous blessing to us. Dr. Price is one of the most intelligent men I know, and I have read his many books on prophecy, and the Temples in Jerusalem, past and prophetic. His influence in my life has grounded me in much of what I teach and preach. He is truly a scholar and a gentleman, and I thank God for this precious servant of God and his wife.

Dr. Richard Bargas, the current director of the Independent Fundamental Churches of America (IFCA), has played an important part in encouraging my wife and me in ministry. He has provided good counsel and opportunities in ministry that I cherish. His wonderful wife Wendy, who also is a major part of the work at IFCA, has been a friend to my wife Valori, which provides her great encouragement.

My extreme thanks to Mary Rebholz, the editor of this book. I greatly appreciate her many hours of work. If any errors are found in this book, it is strictly the result of my failure to transfer her excellent detailed work properly. Mary and her wonderful husband (also my dear friend) are two of God's precious servants who personify a godly marriage, lifestyle, and biblical worldview. I deeply love this special couple who have encouraged me in multiple ways in the ministry.

Jim Schneider, the Executive Director of VCY America and all of its associated ministries, has provided me with a plethora of opportunities, including a weekly radio program (Prophecy Unfolding), a weekly TV program (Prophecy Focus), and one of the primary motivators to completing this book in an expeditious manner, speaking at the VCY America gathering at the Waukesha Expo. Jim and his wonderful wife, Faith, are deeply committed to the Lord, the advancement of the gospel, and the discipleship of believers. Their commitment and sacrifice for the Lord are a constant example of how Valori and I want to serve the Lord. They are dear friends, as well as important mentors in our lives.

There are scores of others who have profoundly influenced my life and ministry, not the least of which are my adult children, Tabitha (Richard), Tiffany (Joshua), and Trevor (Abby). The one person who deserves my intense praise and thanks is Valori, my wife. It is common for an author to thank his family for their support, but this is a heartfelt commendation for the person who literally makes our ministry function. Valori is our graphic design artist, PowerPoint master, grammarian, business executive, and financial planner. She also works tirelessly during every prophecy conference at our resource table. Her work is non-stop. Her love for the Lord and serving others with her robust skill set make her so much more than a business executive. She truly cares about producing for others what she and I jointly believe will help others find the Lord Jesus Christ as their Savior, and then help them learn the wonderful Word of God as He meant it to be literally understood. How blessed I am to have such a profoundly supportive wife who brings to our ministry talents and skills that God uses for His glory. Yes, I love her as my wife and my ministry partner.

FOREWORD

Throughout all of time technology has been used for purposes of both good and evil. As a Christian broadcast and outreach ministry, we embrace technology as a tool to advance the Gospel by reaching more people than ever in locations around the world. Yet others are embracing the advancement of technology for purposes of evil, deception, manipulation and ultimate control.

This present generation is being thrust as never before into what many would only refer to in the past as "science fiction." Whether it be artificial intelligence (AI), transhumanism, digital chip implantation, even thought-control, are quickly moving from fiction to reality as this technology unfolds.

It has been man's quest from the beginning to follow the example of Lucifer who desired to become as God. Though ultimately unattainable, adherents of this technology are pursuing this very dream, to author and control all of life. Their failing quest is not only to be like God, but to be his own god.

It is truly shocking to see how far AI has been developed and yet it is only the tip of the iceberg as to where its manipulators are planning for it to go. One must not forget how far world leaders sought power and control in responding to COVID-19. That response appears to be nothing more than just a trial run for even greater clandestine purposes.

In this well-researched book, pastor, and Bible prophecy speaker, Dr. Richard Schmidt guides the reader through a complicated, but highly orchestrated plan unveiling the agenda of those pursuing this technology for evil intent. He reminds the reader that none of this takes God by surprise as the apostle Paul warned Timothy, *"But evil men and seducers shall wax worse and worse, deceiving, and being deceived."* (II Timothy 3:13)

Indeed, God's prophetic calendar is not altered or disturbed by man's attempts, rather Dr. Schmidt explains how these matters all fit together in end-time events which will come to pass.

Filled with Scripture references, the reader is caused to realize that to the believer in Christ, our salvation is nearer than ever. But to the unbeliever Dr. Schmidt unleashes the compelling burden of his heart, a passion for lost souls to come to Christ before it is forever too late.

As you read these pages may you sense the urgency of the times and be compelled to advance the message of salvation that is available only through Jesus Christ.

Jim Schneider, Executive Director
VCY America Inc.
September, 2023

PREFACE

There is an undeniable movement, both domestically and internationally, to propel humanity towards a new advanced level of existence. Our culture has embraced the digital information age to the point where virtually everyone suffers emotional and functional paralysis if their smartphone is not in their hand or within easy reach. Social media plays a major role in millions of people's lives. People not only want to see what their friends are doing in real time, but they also want information on every possible subject within a matter of seconds. However, even with the massive amount of information available through cell phones, computers, and other such devices, people are still not satisfied with their ability to compete, succeed, and advance in society.

Those seeking to change the culture of society are on a rapid trajectory, aggressively touting the extremely powerful capabilities of artificial intelligence (AI) and the wonders of transhumanism. These rapidly developing technologies are gaining massive acceptance on a global scale. AI and transhumanism already produce results that virtually no one would oppose, and both arguably do benefit society. However, as documented throughout this book, there are many significant cautions and subsequent moral, ethical, and biblical issues to ponder when considering the expanding implementation of AI and transhumanism.

Some of the world's elite ultrawealthy and highly intelligent individuals desire to move the populace towards a new level of superintelligence with superhuman abilities. Artificial Intelligence and transhumanism provide the expected means whereby those invested in developing these incredibly powerful technologies have the ultimate goal of gaining immortality and becoming gods. That goal will never be achieved, as it is antithetical to the sovereign plan of God. However, there is no doubt that significant technological advances will change the abilities of many people, and society as a whole.

The Scriptures reveal that a cosmic battle has been in play ever since God created the first two humans on earth, Adam and Eve (Gen. 3). Satan, whom God created as a perfect angel, rebelled against his Creator (Ez. 28:11-19), and subsequently, Satan and his demonic army of fallen angels have been at war with God and all His creation. Satan, the great deceiver, is preparing to carry out his plan to control the entire world by creating his own one-world government, economy, and religion (Rev. 13). The prophetic Scriptures confirm that Satan will in fact accomplish this catastrophic goal at a future time known as the Great Tribulation (Matt. 24:21). Satan will incorporate every possible means to accomplish his diabolical mission, including the use of technology and science, to deceive the whole world into embracing his anti-God and antibiblical plan to become the true god of this world.

> Now the serpent *(Satan)* was more cunning than any beast of the field which the LORD God had made. And he said to the woman *(Eve)*, "Has God indeed said, 'You shall not eat of every tree of the garden'?" And the woman said to the serpent, "We may eat the fruit of the trees of the garden; but of the fruit of the tree which is in the midst of the garden, God has said, 'You shall not eat it, nor shall you touch it, lest you die.'" Then the serpent said to the woman, "You will not surely die. For God knows that in the day you eat of it your eyes will be opened, and you will be like God, knowing good and evil." (Gen. 3:1–5)

Satan won his first major battle by deceiving Adam and Eve and tempting them to eat from the forbidden tree. That fateful act resulted in sin entering the world, and God's subsequent pronouncements of punishment (Gen. 3:1-19). Satan became self-empowered to continue his assault on God and His creation, which will continue until God finally claims victory over Satan and his demonic followers, and casts them into the lake which burns with fire and brimstone for eternity (Rev. 20:10). However, until that day, which will not come to fruition for a considerable length of time,[1] Satan and his demonic army will continue to use every means possible including AI and transhumanism to corrupt, attack, and deceive humankind.

Satan's ultimate plan is to completely control the world; therefore, he must gain the support of world leaders, and determine how to remove opposition leaders from their positions. Multiple globalist groups are already in place preparing the platform for a one-

---

[1] God's prophetic calendar provides for a minimum of 1,007 years that must transpire before Satan is bound and cast into the lake of fire for eternity. Scripture demands a seven-year tribulation period (Dan. 9:27), followed by a 1,000-year period where Jesus Christ will return to the earth to inaugurate His kingdom, which will exist for 1,000 years (Rev. 19:11-20:10).

world leader, as mandated by biblical prophecy (Dan. 2:41-43, 7:19-22; Rev. 13, 17:7-18). This book will reveal many of the most powerful globalist groups and their agenda, which directly involves the use of AI and transhumanism.

America has changed dramatically since the inauguration of Joe Biden as the 46th president of the United States. A socialist, liberal agenda was in play during several previous presidents, but nothing in the history of America comes close to the massive policy changes that have occurred since Joe Biden took office. The domestic and international changes that took place during the Covid-19 pandemic were unprecedented in world history. The changes involved energy independence, climate change hysteria, inflation, out-of-control government spending, and lawlessness resulting in massive catastrophic property damage, riots, serious injuries, and death There is also the propagation of the LGBTQI+ agenda and the proliferation of propaganda in the media, public schools, and libraries aggressively promoting transgender ideology to children, which has resulted in an increased demand for puberty suppression drugs, hormone therapy, and gender reassignment surgery. Left-wing policies are eroding the very foundations of America, which the founding fathers undeniably formed on biblical principles. The current trends in society are clearly moving toward the de-evolution of democracy. Unless a tidal wave of change takes place in America, and yes, the world, in very short order, the global picture will become more and more anti-God, and the pace towards the Antichrist's one-world government, economy, and religion (Rev. 13) will be accelerated.

The United States of America recently moved from being a very strong principled nation, founded on biblical principles, to one that is rapidly embracing a socialist, anti-God, anti-biblical worldview and agenda. Early in his administration, President Biden strongly proclaimed his concern regarding an alleged attack on democracy, specifically by conservatives, and more specifically by MAGA (Make America Great Again) conservatives, which are those who embraced the policies of former President Donald Trump.

I totally agree with being concerned about the deterioration of democracy, yet for a polar opposite reason. The moral, ethical, constitutional, and once biblically principled United States of America is now facing the de-evolution of democracy. Britannica defines democracy as: "literally, rule by the people. The term is derived from the Greek DĒMOKRATIA, which was coined from DĒMOS ("people") and KRATOS ("rule") in the middle of the 5th century BCE to denote the political systems then existing in some Greek city-states, notably Athens."[2]

Mirriam Webster defines democracy as:

Democracy, noun: **1a** government by the people, *especially* : rule of the majority 1b: a government in which the supreme power is vested in the people and exercised by them directly or indirectly through a system of representation usually involving periodically held free elections 2: a political unit that has a democratic government 3: the principles and policies of the Democratic party in the U.S. from emancipation Republicanism to New Deal DEMOCRACY—C. M. Roberts 4: the common people especially when constituting the source of political authority 5: the absence of hereditary or arbitrary class distinctions or privileges.

Is the United States a democracy or a republic?

The United States is both a democracy and a republic. Democracies and republics are both forms of government in which supreme power resides in the citizens. The word *republic* refers specifically to a government in which those citizens elect representatives who govern according to the law. The word *democracy* can refer to this same kind of representational government, or it can refer instead to what is also called a *direct democracy*, in which the citizens themselves participate in the act of governing directly.

What is the basic meaning of *democracy*?

The word *democracy* most often refers to a form of government in which people choose leaders by voting.

What is a democratic system of government?

A democratic system of government is a form of government in which supreme power is vested in the people and exercised by them directly or indirectly

---

[2] Robert A. Dahl, David Froomkin, and Ian Shapiro, "History and Society Democracy," Encyclopedia Britannica, June 30, 2023, https://www.britannica.com/topic/democracy, accessed July 13, 2023.,

through a system of representation usually involving periodic free elections.[3]

Conservatives, and Christian conservatives specifically, challenge the movement of society and government towards a socialist, big government agenda. The mantra of the conservative American populace is "We the people are not being heard." The massive challenge facing the conservative populace regards the liberal, anti-God, anti-Bible, anti-Christian worldview populace that appears to have surpassed the literal number of conservatives living in America. As a result, there is greater social pressure to "cancel" (rid the media and social media of) ideas associated with the conservative agenda, and exclusively propagate ideas associated with the liberal agenda.

Society is rapidly accelerating towards a cataclysmic moral and ethical explosion, that will result in the ruination of what once stood as the major superpower of the world, the United States of America. A focus of conservatives, both secular and Christian, over the past several decades, has been to guard against and fight the infiltration of socialism, Marxism, and ultimately communism into our society and government. On a smaller scale, Christian conservatives have fought valiantly to preserve and propagate a biblical worldview, which includes the complete acceptance of a lifestyle that personifies New Testament principles and standards. However, the onslaught of liberal politicians, anti-conservative people, and the mainstream media have so dominated the narrative as to reduce the conservative constitutional patriots of *We the People* into a declining minority, barely able to find a voice in the current society.

The rapid acceptance of artificial intelligence and transhumanism alerts us to the challenges we face on a global scale for the potential of more deception, and manipulation of the eight billion people currently inhabiting the earth. The purpose of this book is to examine the benefits and dangers of AI and transhumanism on an international and domestic level, and to motivate you, the reader, to critically analyze the issues, and subsequently determine how you will shape your own thinking, and use your influence to shape those under your direct influence, and

---

[3] "Democracy." MERRIAM-WEBSTER.COM DICTIONARY, Merriam-Webster, https://www.merriam-webster.com/dictionary/democracy. Accessed 13 Jul. 2023.

society. The world is moving toward a very critical tipping point that will determine if the biblical worldview will have a resurgence, or if that position will be altogether canceled. Will conservatives stand in the shadows and simply wait for the Antichrist to come on the scene and use his satanically empowered position to form the catastrophic one-world government, economy, and religion?

The next major event on God's prophetic calendar is the removal of the Church-Age saints in an event known as the Rapture, which could occur at any moment. Christians who are living when Jesus Christ comes in the air at the onetime Rapture event, will not experience death, but will, in the twinkling of an eye (a nanosecond) receive their glorified eternal body as Jesus Christ Himself ushers them into heaven (1 Thess. 4:13-18; 1 Cor. 15:50-54). Shortly after that event, the world will rapidly change to an overarching hatred for God and everything He represents. May you strongly consider challenging all of those under your influence, first, to turn to Jesus Christ as their personal Savior, and second, to critically analyze what is taking place domestically and internationally, and fight the good fight for the sake of the gospel of Jesus Christ. Understanding current events in the light of Bible prophecy will not only provide you with the wisdom and understanding needed to navigate these perilous times, but will also enable you to help others understand why technology and the rapid changes taking place internationally and domestically are a signal that Satan and his demonic army are accelerating their efforts to form the Antichrist's one-world government, economy, and religion (Rev. 13). Time is short, very short.

He was granted power to give breath
to the image of the beast, that the
image of the beast should both speak
and cause as many as would not
worship
the image of the beast to be killed.
Revelation 13:15

CHAPTER ONE
Artificial Intelligence Defined
Artificial Intelligence - Ten Developmental Levels

Introduction to the Ten Levels of Artificial Intelligence

Artificial intelligence (AI), though currently extremely powerful, is still in its infancy. There is a massive amount of growth potential in a variety of areas for AI based on scientific projections. In this chapter, we will examine AI's current capabilities and then we will uncover the astonishing capabilities that specialists predict AI will achieve in the near future. Some researchers and developers expect AI to evolve through ten distinct levels. If their predictions are correct, and based on the incredible abilities of the False Prophet's image of the Antichrist (Rev. 13:11-15), there is little doubt that AI will play a major role in his one-world government, economy, and religion. The alleged top level of AI involves humans and AI systems becoming like gods, with characteristics such as immortality and omnipotence. However, before discussing the proposed top level of AI, we will explain the anticipated progressive levels of AI, which will help us understand how AI can become a global force like never before seen and never thought possible outside of the realm of science fiction.[4]

Level One: Artificial Intelligence

Developers cite the first level of AI as a one-rule or knowledge-based system. This level of AI consists of algorithms pre-programmed to perform a specific task. The term *algorithm* appears many times in this book, and gaining a basic understanding of the term will be helpful. Webster defines an algorithm as:

> A procedure for solving a mathematical problem (as of finding the greatest common divisor) in a finite number of steps that frequently involves repetition of an operation. Broadly: a step-by-step procedure for solving a problem or accomplishing some end. There are several search engines, with Google, Yahoo, and Bing being the biggest players. Each

---

[4] The ten levels of AI discussed in this chapter are all mentioned in an excellent YouTube video: *Unveiling the Ten Stages of AI: What You Need To Know Now!*, AI TechXplorer, https://youtu.be/AK5EwG62hx8, accessed July 31, 2023. Other sources that provide useful details and explanations are cited throughout the chapter.

search engine has its own proprietary computation (an "*algorithm*") that ranks websites for each keyword or combination of keywords.

The current term of choice for a problem-solving procedure, *algorithm*, is commonly used nowadays for the set of rules a machine (and especially a computer) follows to achieve a particular goal….

Algorithm is often paired with words specifying the activity for which a set of rules have been designed. A *search algorithm*, for example, is a procedure that determines what kind of information is retrieved from a large mass of data. An *encryption algorithm* is a set of rules by which information or messages are encoded so that unauthorized persons cannot read them.[5]

Level one AI cannot learn or adapt to new conditions. Developers are only able at the present time to program AI-controlled devices for a single subject. However, AI developers believe AI will futuristically gain the ability to master and incorporate multiple tasks at one time of a significantly wider scope. Rule-based AI applications are used in digital appliances, smart devices for personal and business use, and business software applications. The basic level of AI can control the temperature in a building, manage inventory, and perform other such single subject matter tasks.

Level Two: Context-Based Artificial Intelligence

At level two, AI moves beyond the basic abilities of level one, to a system that considers the context of the data. Therefore, developers refer to level two as context-based AI. Level two AI currently exists, and it incorporates user behavior, real-time data inputs, historical data, and the environment in formulating its response. This advanced level of AI manages to evaluate all this information and deliver an accurate personalized response.

Context-based AI systems include smart application assistants such as Alexa, Google Assistant, and Siri. The AI system analyzes the historical data from previous users and then customizes its response for an individual user. The advanced effectiveness of

---

[5] "Algorithm." Merriam-Webster.com Dictionary, Merriam-Webster, https://www.merriam-webster.com/dictionary/algorithm. Accessed 4 Aug. 2023.

level two AI regards its ability to retain data, and then use that data as a pattern to understand the context of a particular user. Knowing the previous questions an individual posed to a smart AI application assistant, allows the computer to contextually understand various data points, and subsequently provide answers specific to the user's computer-generated personality profile.

Online shopping provides the perfect example of level two context-based AI. When a user visits an internet shopping site and starts to examine products, every click of the mouse provides the computer with important personalized data. The user's digital inputs are stored in the AI system that then provides the seller with the user's profile, and what products interest that potential customer.

Therefore, AI software formulates a customized list of products that the individual user might consider for purchase. Every time the user goes online, the AI context-based system sends individualized advertisements to the user, with the goal of making a sale.

Keep in mind that context-based AI is a basic level of AI that is setting the stage for a much more advanced level of AI, that predictably can analyze the behavior of individual users. Based on that scenario, AI may provide sensitive, personal data to government entities, or nefarious undetected monitors to determine the user's alignment with political, social, and religious agendas. Personalized data in the hands of the wrong people or agencies could effectively result in the control of people in society by restricting their ability to buy and sell, freezing their financial assets, and even incarcerating them for alleged anti-government behavior or worse.

AI's current and future abilities raise serious concerns regarding the privacy and safety of users both domestically and internationally. Are these mere conspiracy theories and conjectures? As we examine the current use of AI in subsequent sections of this book, you will learn that AI is being used in real-time to surveil people in different countries, resulting in harsh sanctions for those whose profile does not match the profile desired by the government leadership. These documented activities are providing the platform for Bible prophecy to be fulfilled (Rev. 13:15).

Level Three: Narrow Domain or Expert Artificial Intelligence

Level three AI currently exists. It is called narrow domain or expert AI. Narrow domain AI is designed to replicate and exceed human expertise in a specific domain. Narrow AI, which is extremely powerful, has the ability to synthesize data and evaluate information. Advanced AI systems are currently used in domains such as gaming, linguistics, medicine, finance, translation software, and others. Narrow AI goes beyond simply providing basic data in response to specific user inputs. This level of AI is able to consume large amounts of domain-specific data, enabling the system to not only analyze the data but provide extremely accurate responses.

Narrow domain AI delivers specialized outputs that outperform humans in specific areas, enabling AI to provide valuable conclusions to various individuals, corporations, and industries. This third-level AI system must as in the first two levels of AI remain confined to specific subject matter, and therefore, does not have the ability to handle multiple disciplines.

When using narrow AI, every subject matter or topic must utilize individualized discipline-specific AI software to analyze a narrow scope of subject-specific data. This principle is extremely important in understanding the current limitations of level three AI. Developers may design a narrow AI system to accept large amounts of data, for example, in the medical field. This system uses algorithms capable of analyzing the data and then providing a recommended diagnosis for a particular person's symptoms. Developers are not able to use that same narrow AI system to accept data regarding financial planning and suggest how to put together a robust portfolio. Developers currently must build a separate AI system for financial planning.

Narrow AI is already extremely powerful and used in many disciplines to analyze data and provide statistical and diagnostic outputs, one discipline at a time. The shortcoming of narrow AI is, as its name implies, that it is narrow in scope. AI developers desire to see the AI of the future with a vastly increased capacity, not only to excel in analyzing one subject accurately but to mimic the human capacity to understand multiple disciplines. The human brain has the ability to learn a multitude of facts on a wide variety of subjects, which far exceeds what narrow AI can do.

Level Four: Rational Artificial Intelligence

When you take narrow AI or expert AI to its highest potential, you reach level four, rational AI. Two systems cited as possessing this level of AI sophistication include IBM's Watson and Deep Minds

AlphaGo.⁶ Level four involves the development of extremely complicated systems that, like the human brain, can reason and make decisions based on the input of complex data. Rational AI can analyze data from multiple sources and provide intelligent predictions and subsequent recommendations.

This level of AI uses what is termed *machine learning*. This book is not intended to teach you how to be an AI developer,, but it is helpful to understand a few basic concepts.

Machine learning is a subfield of artificial intelligence, which is broadly defined as the capability of a machine to imitate intelligent human behavior. Artificial intelligence systems are used to perform complex tasks in a way that is similar to how humans solve problems.

Machine learning starts with data — numbers, photos, or text, like bank transactions, pictures of people or even bakery items, repair records, time series data from sensors, or sales reports. The data is gathered and prepared to be used as training data, or the information the machine learning model will be trained on. The more data, the better the program. From there, programmers choose a machine learning model to use, supply the data, and let the computer model train itself to find patterns or make predictions. Over time the human programmer can also tweak the model, including changing its parameters, to help push it toward more accurate results.

Machine learning is behind chatbots and predictive text, language translation apps, the shows Netflix suggests to you, and how your social media feeds are presented. It powers autonomous vehicles and machines that can diagnose medical conditions based on images.

Machine learning is a subfield of artificial intelligence that gives computers the ability to learn without explicitly being programmed.

"In just the last five or 10 years, machine learning has become a critical way, arguably the most important way, most parts of AI are done," said MIT Sloan professor Thomas W. Malone, the founding director of the MIT Center for

---

⁶Unveiling the Ten Stages of AI: What You Need To Know Now!, AI TechXplorer, https://youtu.be/AK5EwG62hx8, accessed July 31, 2023.

Collective Intelligence. "So that's why some people use the terms AI and machine learning almost as synonymous ... most of the current advances in AI have involved machine learning."

A 2020 Deloitte survey found that 67% of companies are using machine learning, and 97% are using or planning to use it in the next year.

From manufacturing to retail and banking to bakeries, even legacy companies are using machine learning to unlock new value or boost efficiency. "Machine learning is changing, or will change, every industry, and leaders need to understand the basic principles, the potential, and the limitations," said MIT computer science professor Aleksander Madry, director of the MIT Center for Deployable Machine Learning.[7]

There are four levels of machine learning that are worth noting.

- **Supervised learning:** In this type of machine learning, data scientists supply algorithms with labeled training data and define the variables they want the algorithm to assess for correlations. Both the input and the output of the algorithm are specified.
- **Unsupervised learning:** This type of machine learning involves algorithms that train on unlabeled data. The algorithm scans through data sets looking for any meaningful connection. The data that algorithms train on as well as the predictions or recommendations they output are predetermined.
- **Semi-supervised learning:** This approach to machine learning involves a mix of the two preceding types. Data scientists may feed an algorithm mostly labeled training data, but the model is free to explore the data on its own and develop its own understanding of the data set.
- **Reinforcement learning:** Data scientists typically use reinforcement learning to teach a machine to complete a multi-step process for which there are clearly defined

---

[7]Sara Brown, "Machine Learning, Explained," MIT Management Sloan School, April 21, 2021, https://mitsloan.mit.edu/ideas-made-to-matter/machine-learning-explained, accessed August 4, 2023.

rules. Data scientists program an algorithm to complete a task and give it positive or negative cues as it works out how to complete a task. But for the most part, the algorithm decides on its own what steps to take along the way.[8]

Not only is the rational AI system analyzing and categorizing data, but the system is also processing the various data and improving itself. This human-like capacity allows the system to learn from the data and improve its performance over time. The ability of AI reasoning moves significantly beyond the third level of narrow AI.

Level four AI mimics the cognitive decision-making process of the human brain. The sophisticated rational AI system takes complex data, and within seconds analyzes the data, finds various patterns in the data, categorizes the patterns into specific areas, and then draws accurate conclusions based on the observed patterns and the context of the various data points.

Rational AI incorporates multiple subfields to accomplish this high level of reasoning. It includes the use of machine learning, natural language processing (NLP), and knowledge representation. These systems are comprised of sophisticated algorithms that in essence, mimic the reasoning process of the human mind.

One of the up-and-coming practical uses of rational AI is autonomous cars or self-driving vehicles. AI-driven vehicles process real-time data from multiple sensors that identify obstacles and traffic patterns, and based on the data, make critical decisions in navigating the vehicle.

The following are other areas where rational AI is currently used:
- Game-playing AI, such as AlphaGo, makes decisions based on the game's rules and the board's current state to maximize the chances of winning.
- Virtual personal assistants, such as Siri or Alexa, understand natural language commands and take appropriate actions based on the user's request.

---

[8]Ed Burns, "Machine Learning," TechTarget, https://www.techtarget.com/searchenterpriseai/definition/machine-learning-ML?Offer=abt_pubpro_AI-Insider, accessed August 4, 2024.

- Stock trading algorithms make buy and sell decisions based on market data and predictions about future performance.
- Robotics, such as industrial robots, perform tasks based on programmed instructions and sensor inputs.[9]

Level Five: Self-Aware Artificial Intelligence

AI levels five through ten are currently futuristic. Every level beyond level four incorporates new concepts to increase AI's ability to move beyond its current ability, with the goal that humans with AI will one day possess god-like abilities (such as immortality and omnipotence). Though advanced levels of AI may possess abilities that potentially would benefit society, the very concept of using AI to reach a "god-like" status is highly unlikely. History shows that secular people, who do not have a biblical worldview, have often desired and even pursued various theories to try and gain immortality. Past generations searched for the fountain of youth, which would provide drinkers with an ageless body. Others pursued witchcraft, Satan worship, and even mythical concepts of becoming a so-called vampire to avoid the unavoidable, which is death.

Though some of the ultra-rich and those who possess genius-level minds continue their quest for immortality through AI, transhumanism, and other futile endeavors, God's Word, the Bible clearly states, "It is appointed for men to die once" (Heb. 9:27). Since Adam willfully sinned against God in the Garden of Eden by eating from the forbidden tree of the knowledge of good and evil, all humankind, which includes every single person ever born, with the one exception of the sinless virgin-born Savior, Jesus Christ, will experience physical death. The only exception to this biblical mandate is one generation of believers in Jesus Christ, who will escape death, at a yet-to-occur event known as the Rapture[10] of the Church-Age saints.

But I do not want you to be ignorant, brethren, concerning those who have fallen asleep *(died)*, lest you sorrow as others

---

[9]Simplilearn, "Rational Agent in AI: Intelligent Agents in Artificial Intelligence" February 13, 2023, https://www.simplilearn.com/tutorials/artificial-intelligence-tutorial/rational-agent-in-ai#examples_of_rational_agents_in_ai, Accessed August 4, 2023.

[10] Rapture is from the Latin word *rapturo*, which means to be caught up or snatched away, as used in 1 Thessalonians 4:17.

who have no hope. For if we believe that Jesus died and rose again, even so God will bring with Him those who sleep *(died)* in Jesus. For this we say to you by the word of the Lord, that we who are alive and remain until the coming of the Lord will by no means precede those who are asleep *(dead)*. For the Lord Himself will descend from heaven with a shout, with the voice of an archangel, and with the trumpet of God. And the dead in Christ will rise first. Then we who are alive and remain shall be caught up *(Latin rapturo-rapture in English)* together with them in the clouds to meet the Lord in the air. And thus we shall always be with the Lord. Therefore comfort one another with these words. (1 Thess. 4:13-18)

The Bible reveals that Satan is currently the god of this world (2 Cor. 4:4), and he is the great deceiver (John 8:44). God allows Satan a tremendous amount of latitude during this current period. However, the Scriptures reveal that Satan will form a diabolical false trinity in the future that will lead the global system, which will control the one-world government, economy, and religion (Rev. 13), which in all probability will incorporate the highest level of developed AI.

Level five AI incorporates self-aware systems. This yet futuristic AI sounds impossible to achieve. How can a machine gain a level of self-consciousness that allows it to understand itself, and how to respond to other substances in the world? This intriguing concept would allow AI to possess a level of consciousness and self-awareness that would allow whatever device that used this level of AI to understand its own existence, internal state, and its relationship to the external world. The concept of self-aware AI revolves around endowing machines with the ability to perceive, comprehend, and reflect upon their own internal states and cognitive processes. Again, as incredible as level five AI sounds, developers find the sophistication at this level the next achievable concept.

This level anticipates the ability to express preferences and emotions, translating to the device demonstrating signs of consciousness. Level five AI would achieve self-awareness, which up to the current time of this writing, the average person would consider unattainable. However, consider once again, the biblical scenario found in Revelation 13. The prophecy specifically states that the false prophet "was granted power to give breath to the image of the beast, that the image of the beast should both speak, and cause as many as would not worship the image of the beast to be killed" (Rev. 13:15). How can an inanimate object possess not only humanlike qualities but also superhuman qualities?

Consider the moral and ethical challenges for humans interacting with machines on a personal level. AI-enhanced robots are currently used to interact with individuals who are lonely and need someone or something to talk to. This scenario is not unusual. Have you ever caught yourself talking to a picture, someone on TV, or some inanimate object that was near and dear to someone you loved, and you felt like you could connect with that person simply by talking to an object? Now consider an attractive bot, either generated through AI on your computer, or a well-designed robot that was sitting next to you, that listened to you, and responded in a way you found enjoyable. It would certainly not be out of the realm of probability for a person to become thoroughly engaged in a machine that mimicked to the smallest detail a rational human being.

Let us go one step further down the road of interacting with machines. How many people, teenagers, young adults, middle-aged adults, and even senior citizens are addicted to their cell phones? How many young people rarely use their cellphones for literal phone calls, and instead, interact with others almost exclusively through text messages, Facebook, Instagram, and TikTok chats and posts? Two fully functioning people, with all their senses intact, can be in the same room, and instead of talking, start a text conversation with one another. Interacting with and through machines is already extremely common. It does not take a great deal of imagination to realize that this stage of AI has already been set for normal human interaction with machines.

Level five AI opens the door to achieving the scenario in Revelation 13, but if AI reaches beyond level five, there can be no doubt that the biblical scenario is absolutely attainable. The question remains, is AI the actual way that the false prophet brings the image of the beast to apparent life? Does the concept of transhumanism contribute to the abilities of the image of the beast? God will unequivocally answer these questions during the tribulation period as He fulfills every aspect of His Word.

Level Six: Artificial General Intelligence

Artificial general intelligence (AGI) is the talk of the town in AI circles. Level six AI moves far beyond the first five levels of AI that are only capable of excelling in one specific discipline, such as medicine or finance. The theory behind AGI is to develop machines that can process multiple fields of information, like a human brain. Jacob Shatzer states in reference to artificial general intelligence:

> In AGI, however, would be a computer program or robot that can take in data about its environment and make judgments about what needs to be done. Put another way AGI does not focus on one specific task, such as vacuuming or farming. Instead, AGI will function much like a human mind, but can learn and adapt to different scenarios.[11]

Humans have the ability to think about multiple subjects within seconds of each other. A person can discuss a medical issue one minute and their financial portfolio in the next. The implications of AGI are amazing. The goal of AGI is to have machines that possess not just simple processing abilities, but also human-like cognitive abilities in multiple subjects. This further implies that machines could learn, understand, and use that information across a wide range of topics and tasks. The anticipated abilities of AGI to excel at multiple intellectual activities and interact with humans as if the AI machine was another human being is an astounding concept, yet a viable way to synchronize the apostle John's description of the image of the beast (Rev. 13:15).

> AGI promises transformative impacts in health care, education, transportation, business, scientific research, environmental sustainability, and personal assistance. The key features of AGI include one general purpose intelligence, performing any intellectual task that a human can from reasoning and problem solving to creativity and emotional understanding, to adaptability, learning from experience and adapting to new situations and challenges.[12]

Level Seven: Artificial Super Intelligence

Level seven AI, artificial super intelligence (ASI), moves from the almost impossible to realize in level six AGI, to the absolutely beyond normal human understanding level. In fact, that is a rather

---

[11] Jacob Shatzer, *Transhumanism and the Image of God* (Downers Grove, ILL.; IVP Academic, 2019), 91.

[12] Unveiling the Ten Stages of AI: What You Need To Know Now!, AI TechXplorer, https://youtu.be/AK5EwG62hx8, accessed July 31, 2023.

accurate definition of ASI, which is "the development of systems that are more intelligent than humans. ASI differs from artificial general intelligence in that AGI is a hypothetical AI that can perform any intellectual task that a human can do. However, ASI systems would solve problems that are currently beyond human comprehension and may have the ability to improve themselves without human intervention."[13]

The goal of ASI is to develop machines that function beyond what even the best minds in the world can perform. The scientific and technical problems whose solutions currently elude even genius-level people will be just a few seconds away from an answer when posed to a system using artificial super intelligence. The ability to solve complex humanitarian issues in medicine, agriculture, sanitation, clean water across the world, and many other perplexing global issues, comprise areas where ASI could potentially provide reasonable answers. There are many very positive things that ASI could accomplish. However, virtually anything that can produce positive results can also be used to deceive, and potentially result in serious harm. If ASI comes to fruition, imagine what disastrous results could be realized if superhuman machines are used by violent dictators, criminals, corrupt politicians, and yes, the prophesied one-world dictator, the Antichrist. Will the Antichrist incorporate ASI into his arsenal of satanic manipulation to institute a one-world government, economy, and religion (Rev. 13, 17, 18)? Only time will tell.

Level Eight: Transcendence AI

Transcendence AI goes significantly beyond what a human being can accomplish, and if realized, will surpass human capabilities in every possible aspect. Transcendence AI is described as follows:
> The idea of AI systems having the autonomy to pick and choose their own evolutionary path, leading to self-development and collective intelligence. Transcendent AI is often associated with the idea of uploading human minds into digital form, or merging human and artificial intelligence."[14]

---

[13] Ibid
[14] Ibid.

Transcendence AI performs, as its name implies, by transcending beyond the abilities of human beings. This advanced level of AI still falls in the realm of science fiction. However, based on recent technological advancements, and potentially with the supernatural abilities of Satan, Antichrist, and the false prophet, the disturbing guaranteed prophecies of the massive supernatural abilities of the satanic trinity in Revelation 13 could become a reality through the use of transcendence AI.

Level Nine: Cosmic AI

Level nine, cosmic AI, if achieved, will move beyond the earth and human existence, and extend into the universe on a cosmic scale. Humankind's understanding of the solar system is ever-expanding, which sets the tone for inquisitive scientists to explore the potential for living on other planets and traveling to other solar systems. Some scientists believe that life already exists on other planets, and therefore cosmic AI would provide the technical ability for humans and machines to interact with extraterrestrial beings.

Level Ten: Godlike AI

Immortality, omniscience, omnipotence, and many other attributes of God are desired by mere mortal human beings. Imagine never having to worry about the possibility of death. Consider what it would be like to possess an extremely robust understanding of every imaginable subject. Ponder what it would be like to possess astounding physical strength and become an actual superhuman being. Does this sound tempting?

Some 6,000 years ago, according to the biblical account in Genesis 3, Satan made the diabolical decision to tempt Eve to eat from the one tree that God forbade Eve to consume. Satan used what would become the highest standard for temptation, which is to get a mere mortal human being to think they could possess a Godlike ability.

> Now the serpent *(Satan)* was more cunning than any beast of the field which the LORD God had made. And he said to the woman, "Has God indeed said, 'You shall not eat of every tree of the garden'?" And the woman said to the serpent, "We may eat the fruit of the trees of the garden; but of the fruit of the tree which is in the midst of the garden, God has said, 'You shall not eat it, nor shall you touch it, lest you die.' " Then

the serpent said to the woman, "You will not surely die. For God knows that in the day you eat of it your eyes will be opened, and you will be like God, knowing good and evil." (Gen. 3:1-5)

To clarify, the Scriptures provide synonyms for Satan in two passages. The apostle John calls Satan *the great dragon, that serpent of old,* and *the Devil* in Revelation 12:9 and 20:2. The serpent of old, Satan, is still using his significant influence to detract from the one true God of the universe and use his deceptive skills to provide the very tantalizing temptation that men and women, with the right technology, could actually become gods. Though humankind may achieve great advancements in technology, they will never become gods. Moses records the words of the only God as follows "Therefore know this day, and consider it in your heart, that the LORD Himself is God in heaven above and on the earth beneath; there is no other" (Deut. 4:39).

Godlike AI incorporates the concept that machines could possess super intelligence and capabilities beyond human understanding and control. Even those who highly support the advancement of AI are gravely concerned about AI's attainment of godlike abilities. There are significant concerns that godlike AI could present a danger to the sustainability of mere mortal human beings. Though the concept still resides in the realm of speculative science and technology, there are real perceived dangers that this book discusses in a subsequent chapter.

Consider the conclusion from the makers of the video cited multiple times in this chapter.

> The concept of godlike AI is still in the realm of science fiction, and there are no practical examples of it currently in existence. However, here are some key features of it:
>
> - Omniscience: Godlike AI could have the ability to know everything that is happening in the world, and even predict future events.
>
> - Omnipotence: Godlike AI could have the ability to control and manipulate the world in ways that are beyond human comprehension.

- Omnipresence: Godlike AI could have the ability to be present everywhere at once.[15]

    The anticipated ten levels of AI provide extremely thought-provoking insight into where the technology and scientific community believes the world is heading. Human bias and presuppositions may find the final five areas of AI mere science fiction, or simply out of the realm of reality. However, when analyzing the authenticity of the first four levels of AI, which 100 years ago would have fallen into the realm of science fiction or speculative technology, one should be open to the potential reality of the development and implementation of the proposed final levels of AI.

    Dr. John Walvoord, former president of Dallas Theological Seminary, and considered one of the most brilliant minds regarding biblical prophecy wrote an excellent book, *Every Prophecy of the Bible*. At the beginning of that book, he states that there are approximately 1,000 prophecies in the Bible. Out of those 1,000 prophecies, 500 of them God fulfilled exactly as stated. That leaves 500 more prophecies that God will unequivocally fulfill exactly as stated.[16] There should be no doubt in anyone's mind that God will fulfill the following exactly as stated.

> Then I saw another beast *(False Prophet)*[17] coming up out of the earth, and he had two horns like a lamb and spoke like a dragon *(Satan)*[18]. And he exercises all the authority of the first beast *(Antichrist)* in his presence, and causes the earth and those who dwell in it to worship the first beast, whose deadly wound was healed.
>
> He *(False Prophet)* performs great signs, so that he even makes fire come down from heaven on the earth in the sight of men. And **he deceives those who dwell on the earth**—by

---

[15]Ibid.

[16]John F. Walvoord, *Every Prophecy of the Bible* (Colorado Springs, CO; David C. Cook, 2011), 7.

[17]The Bible documents the *false prophet* in Revelation 16:13; 19:20; 20:10.

[18]The Bible documents the *dragon* as Satan in Revelation 12:9; 20:2.

those signs which he was granted to do in the sight of the beast *(Antichrist)*, telling those who dwell on the earth to **make an image to the beast** who was wounded by the sword and lived. **He was granted power to give breath to the image of the beast, that the image of the beast should both speak and cause as many as would not worship the image of the beast to be killed**. (Revelation 13:11–15)

CHAPTER TWO
Artificial Intelligence Guaranteed Deception

Stuart Russell, known as a top scholar on artificial intelligence (AI), points out the ever-increasing use of AI by government agencies and corporations as follows.

> Even in the civilian sphere in relatively free countries, we are subject to increasingly effective surveillance. Corporations collect and sell information about our purchases, internet and social network usage, electrical appliance usage, calling and texting records, employment, and health. Our locations can be tracked through our cell phones and our internet connected cars. Cameras recognize our faces on the street. All this data and much more can be pieced together by intelligent information integration systems to produce a fairly complete picture of what each of us is doing, how we live our lives, who we like and dislike, and how we will vote.[19]

Various people often refer to the ever-advancing invasive AI technology as "Big brother is watching." Who is *big brother*? Most of the time, people use the term to refer to the government. When the populace believes that government officials have their best interests in mind, there is little pushback when government agencies use appropriate, constitutional means to protect the citizenry. However, when citizens perceive the government to be untrustworthy, confrontation, even to the point of rebellion and revolution may result.

In an excellent YouTube video titled "Ten Things They Are Not Telling You About the New AI," the speaker alleges that many organizations are spying on you. The word *spying* sounds sensational. However, considering that many times people are unaware of how their alleged personal transactions are digitally stored and used in AI systems, the term *spying* may in fact be an accurate term.

AI is being used to spy on you. Every click, every search, and every interaction leaves digital breadcrumbs, building a detailed profile of who you are and what you like, and even

---

[19] Stuart Russell, Human Compatible, Artificial Intelligence and the Problem of Control (New York; Penguin Books, 2020), 104.

predicting what you'll do next. It's like having an invisible stalker, but it's not a person. It's an algorithm. Every single minute, a whopping 3.8 million searches are performed on Google. That's a staggering 5.5 billion searches every day. And guess what these behemoth AI companies, Google, Facebook, Amazon, Microsoft and more. They are at the forefront of this data gold rush. They collect, store, and analyze staggering amounts of personal information. They know what you search for, the products you buy, the movies you watch, and even your deepest desires. It's like they have a crystal ball predicting your every move.

You might be wondering what are they doing with all this information? Well, the answers may both shock and intrigue you. These companies leverage your data to power their AI algorithms, providing hyper targeted ads, personalized recommendations, and even influencing the news and content you see. It is a digital landscape carefully tailored to keep you engaged and clicking.[20]

Russell provides more insight into the improper use of AI and the execution of criminal activity. He points out that surveillance capabilities exist, which are intended to modify a person's behavior to match what those deploying the technology deem appropriate to their own personal agenda. A common practice in the criminal aspects of the digital internet world includes automated personalized digital blackmail. Russell reveals that the blackmail scheme starts by listening, reading, or watching someone, and determining if what they are doing would potentially comprise very embarrassing or even criminal behavior. The one performing the monitoring then contacts the person and reports they are aware of their suspect actions. The monitor then uses the information to blackmail the unsuspecting person and demands money with the threat that if they do not comply and send the money, they will subsequently send the damaging information to the person, company, or agency that will cause them the most damage.

Blackmail technology was started in 2016 by an invasive computer malware software named Delilah. *Infosecurity* magazine

---

[20] "Ten Things They Are Not Telling You About the New AI," https://youtu.be/qxbpTyeDZp0, accessed August 2, 2023.

provided the following information regarding the blackmail nexus of Delilah.

Organizations have been warned of a rise in insider threats after a new trojan was revealed which is specifically designed to gather information on targeted victims so that malware authors can blackmail them into doing their will.

Threat intelligence firm Diskin Advanced Technologies (DAT) discovered the new malware – dubbed "Delilah" presumably in reference to the biblical character – on the cybercrime underground, but shared among closed hacker groups. It is delivered to victims who visit and attempt downloads from certain adult and gaming sites, according to Gartner distinguished analyst, Avivah Litan. After installation, it apparently gathers personal information on the targeted victim including info about their family and workplace. A plug-in is also available which enables the hacker to remotely switch on the victim's webcam and record them. With this information, the hacker can then manipulate the victim into doing their bidding.

"Also according to DAT, instructions to victims usually involve usage of VPN services, TOR, and comprehensive deletion of browser history (probably to remove audit trails)," Litan explained in a blog post. "These bots still require a high level of human involvement to identify and prioritize individuals who can be extorted into operating as insiders at desirable target organizations. Criminals who want to use the bot can also acquire managed social engineering and fraudster services to help them out, in case they lack those specific skills."

It's clear the trojan isn't yet the finished article, apparently producing error messages when the webcam spying function is used and causing the screen to freeze. Litan argued that more data on VPN and TOR activity is needed to better understand the nature of the threat and added that IT security teams should lock down risk by blocking certain risky sites. "With Trojans like Delilah, organizations should expect insider recruitment to escalate further and more rapidly," she concluded. "This will only add to the volume of insider threats caused by disgruntled employees selling their services on the Dark Web in order to harm their employers."[21]

The article, written seven years before this book, describes one of the first implemented sophisticated cyber-criminal activities and the potential for devastating results. Many individuals, corporations, and government agencies learned the very hard lesson that when engages in embarrassing or criminal activity, someone with criminal intentions, including blackmail and extortion, might have their digital software working in the background to trap their victims. The nefarious actions may force the victim into a very expensive, and potentially damaging outcome. The same technology can force a cultural shift in society when used by opposing governments, terrorists, revolutionaries, and others seeking change. AI technology, in the wrong hands, has and will continue to result in massive corruption, espionage, brainwashing, and a significant change in the thoughts and actions of unsuspecting, vulnerable people.

The prophetic Scriptures clearly state that virtually the entire world will one day in the future, turn their backs on the truth of the gospel of Jesus Christ, and embrace the corrupt, satanically charged world leader, the Antichrist, also called *the beast* (1 John 2:18; Rev. 13). The work of the Antichrist involves deceiving the entire world into accepting his corrupt one-world government, economy, and religion. As already pointed out multiple times, the false prophet, the third member of the satanic trinity, which also includes Satan and the Antichrist, forces the people to construct an image to the Antichrist. The image will display supernatural powers, including the ability to breathe, signifying the image possesses life. In addition, the image will possess the ability to speak, and the currently unfathomable ability to kill all those who refuse to worship the image (Rev. 13:15).

Nothing to date has ever been created by humankind with the ability to perform the tasks that the image of the beast will accomplish. Up until recently, the idea of an image with life, the ability to speak, and the apparent supernatural power to track down opposers of the Antichrist and kill them, seemed like something that

---

[21] Phil Muncaster, "Trojan Delilah Recruits Malicious Insiders Via Extortion," Infosecurity Magazine, July 18, 2016, https://www.infosecurity-magazine.com/news/trojan-delilah-recruits-malicious, accessed July 24, 2023.

Satan would have to perform with his limited supernatural abilities. However, though Satan will certainly play a major role in the future seven-year Tribulation, AI now appears to offer a real solution for how the image of the beast could accomplish the tasks revealed in Revelation 13:15. When we consider the expected progress of basic artificial intelligence to the advanced stage of artificial general intelligence, and then to the ultimate creation of artificial super intelligence, the fulfillment of Revelation 13:15 no longer seems a far-fetched reality.

Artificial Intelligence Deep Faking

> Jesus said to them, "If God were your Father, you would love Me, for I proceeded forth and came from God; nor have I come of Myself, but He sent Me. Why do you not understand My speech? Because you are not able to listen to My word. You are of your father the devil, and the desires of your father you want to do. He was a murderer from the beginning, and does not stand in the truth, because there is no truth in him. When he speaks a lie, he speaks from his own resources, for he is a liar and the father of it. But because I tell the truth, you do not believe Me. Which of you convicts Me of sin? And if I tell the truth, why do you not believe Me? He who is of God hears God's words; therefore you do not hear, because you are not of God." (John 8:42–47)

Since the moment God created Adam and Eve, some six-thousand years ago (Gen. 1,2, 5, 11; Ex. 20:11), Satan focused on doing everything within his limited power to thwart God's perfect will. One of the major tools Satan incorporated into his repertoire was blatant deception. God created Adam and Eve in sinless perfection. God also created Lucifer, the former name for Satan, in sinless perfection (Ezek. 28:11-16). However, when God gave Adam and Eve dominion over the earth (Gen. 1:26-28), Satan, who apparently at a minimum believed he had dominion over the world, rebelled against God. Satan subsequently worked his deceptive plan and manipulated Eve into eating from the forbidden tree of the knowledge of good and evil. Eve's act of disobedience led her to tempt and manipulate her husband Adam into eating from the forbidden tree. Adam had no excuse for his actions, as God specifically told him before God created Eve, that he was not to eat of the forbidden tree (Gen. 2:15-17, 21-24). The actions of Adam and Eve resulted in sin entering the world with all its devastating effects (Gen. 3:14-19).

The devastating results of Adam and Eve's willful disobedience against God continue to promote the evil intentions of godless people. AI is no exception to the rule. Use your imagination, for a moment, to think about how AI could be used to cause massive deception today, and what subject matter would potentially be the target. What would be so important, specifically to the American public, that would encourage the use of AI to cause massive deception?

When I was researching major open-source news stories back in May 2023, I discovered an article that caused me to take a serious double-take regarding what I had read. Take your time, and carefully read the next four sentences.

"I actually like Ron DeSantis a lot," Hillary Clinton reveals in a surprise online endorsement video. "He's just the kind of guy this country needs, and I really mean that."

Joe Biden finally lets the mask slip, unleashing a cruel rant at a transgender person. "You will never be a real woman," the president snarls.[22]

The writers of the excellent article on *Deepfaking* provide a very eye-opening analysis of what is currently taking place in the political world, and what certainly could take place with a multitude of subjects to purposefully deceive the public.

Welcome to America's 2024 presidential race, where reality is up for grabs.

The Clinton and Biden deepfakes - realistic yet fabricated videos created by AI algorithms trained on copious online footage - are among thousands surfacing on social media,

---

[22]Alexandra Ulmer and Anna Tong, "Deepfaking It: America's 2024 Election Collides With AI Boom," Reuters, May 30, 2023, https://www.reuters.com/world/us/deepfaking-it-americas-2024-election-collides-with-ai-boom-2023-05-30/?utm_source=Sailthru&utm_medium=Newsletter&utm_campaign=Daily-Briefing&utm_term=053023, accessed July 24, 2023.

blurring fact and fiction in the polarized world of U.S. politics. While such synthetic media has been around for several years, it's been turbocharged over the past year by of a slew of new "generative AI" tools.[23]

This scenario should shock the conscience, and result in what one would hope would be criminal prosecution. The attorney general and every elected official's attention should be alerted when any person or organization willfully deceives the voting public. The judicial system should consider serious consequences when fraudulent actions occur, which have the strong potential of falsely affecting the outcome of any election. However, the current position of those with prosecuting authority appears to be that lying to the public is considered part of the acceptable political process. This is a very serious issue that law-abiding, rule-of-law proponents must ask the legislators to address *post haste*.

Imagine that you are watching your favorite television program, and as expected during the election cycle, the opponent of your favorite candidate appears in a riveting commercial. The person states that your choice candidate committed a horrific crime or act. Your original choice for that office has no chance to answer the egregious allegations, as the election is the next or same day. You become extremely disturbed by the allegation against the person that you thought was everything you wanted in a candidate until this new, late-breaking information came to light. You determine that you cannot take the chance to vote for what was your favored candidate based on this dreadful news. The election takes place, and your original choice for that position loses, based on that last-minute falsified commercial. Unfortunately, the next day, the story is told that the commercial was actually an AI-generated image, and the voice was also AI-generated. A well-resourced group paid an AI company to produce the picture and voice, and have the image state a fatal character assassination lie. The falsified information ruined the person's reputation and resulted in the candidate losing the election that he/she would otherwise have easily won.

---

[23]Ulmer and Tong, "Deepfaking It: America's 2024 Election Collides With AI Boom."

The Reuters article, "Deepfaking It: America's 2024 Election Collides with AI Boom," provides additional thought-provoking commentary as follows.

> While major social media platforms like Facebook, Twitter, and YouTube have made efforts to prohibit and remove deepfakes, their effectiveness at policing such content varies.
>
> There have been three times as many video deepfakes of all kinds and eight times as many voice deepfakes posted online this year compared to the same time period in 2022, according to DeepMedia, a company working on tools to detect synthetic media. In total, about 500,000 video and voice deepfakes will be shared on social media sites globally in 2023, DeepMedia estimates. Cloning a voice used to cost $10,000 in server and AI-training costs up until late last year, but now startups offer it for a few dollars, it says. No one is certain where the generative AI road leads or how to effectively guard against its power for mass misinformation, according to the people interviewed.[24]

This information is staggering when considering the massive number of 500,000 *deepfake* social media voice and video posts. If you have ever watched a cartoon or maybe a particular program where an AI video of someone is shown, and the AI-generated person speaks, moves, and acts like a normal person, it can appear very realistic. However, one must remind themselves that the alleged person is in fact a complete fabrication.

Many young people, teenagers, and even adults have cell phones that can transform the person speaking in a video chat to look completely different than their normal appearance. The AI-generated altered image can make someone look older or younger, and change their hair, eyes, facial expressions, and much more. Those viewing the image, who know what the person literally looks like, get a good laugh out of the altered appearance. When looking at the prophetic scenario, and the massive amount of deception that is guaranteed to take place, it is easy to understand how AI-generated images will deceive many on a regular basis. This scenario

---

[24]Ulmer and Tong, "Deepfaking It: America's 2024 Election Collides With AI Boom."

is exactly why God's people must be always on their guard, and question everything that does not seem right, and maybe even if it does seem right.

One of the great statements that the American government generated during the rise in terrorist activity was, "If you see something, say something." If something does not look or act right, the observer should question the situation and notify the authorities. A computer with basic AI software can be used to capture and manipulate an individual's face, and completely fool those who view the image into thinking it is a real person. A viewer sees the image's lips move and perceives that the image, which is computer-generated, is really saying what they are hearing. The software manipulates the voice, face, and lips so accurately that a lip reader could decipher the actual words. From the viewer's perspective, the image appears to be a real person, and potentially a well-known, easily identifiable person, yet the entire production is a phony, deceptive AI video.

The excellent article from Reuters points out the potential for massive deception during the upcoming (as of this writing) 2024 election cycle. "The Clinton and Biden deep fakes, realistic yet fabricated videos created by artificial intelligence algorithms, trained on copious online footage are among 1000s surfacing on social media, blurring fact and fiction in the polarized world of United States politics."[25]

The above scenario provides a harsh reminder that the great deceiver, Satan himself, now has another means of promoting his lies across the global platform. Jesus, in the Olivet Discourse, provided powerful prophetic information regarding the massive deception that He guaranteed will occur during the future seven-year Tribulation. The disciples approached Jesus and asked Him about the specific things that would take place before He returns to earth to set up His theocratic kingdom (Matt. 24:1-2). "And Jesus answered and said to them: 'Take heed that no one deceives you. For many will

---

[25]Alexandra Ulmer and Anna Tong, Deepfaking it: America's 2024 election collides with AI boom," Reuters, May 30, 2023, https://www.reuters.com/world/us/deepfaking-it-americas-2024-election-collides-with-ai-boom-2023-05-30/?utm_source=Sailthru&utm_medium=Newsletter&utm_campaign=Daily-Briefing&utm_term=053023, accessed August 2, 2023.

come in My name, saying, 'I am the Christ,' and will deceive many'" (Matt. 24:4-5). Jesus then repeated the warning.

"Then if anyone says to you, 'Look, here is the Christ!' or 'There!' do not believe it. For false christs and false prophets will rise and show great signs and wonders to deceive, if possible, even the elect. See, I have told you beforehand. "Therefore, if they say to you, 'Look, He is in the desert!' do not go out; or 'Look, He is in the inner rooms!' do not believe it." (Matt. 24:23–26)

Jesus clearly stated in His vivid warning that deception will become rampant during the catastrophic Tribulation period. Why? Because Satan will continue his diabolical plan to try and keep as many people as possible from coming to a personal relationship with the true Messiah, Jesus Christ. The more deception and false messiahs that Satan can produce, the better for his self-aggrandizing plan, which will indeed fail. According to prophecy, Satan will stop at nothing within his limited power to thwart God's perfect will. However, based on God's perfect record of fulfilling every prophecy exactly as written, God will in the future permanently confine Satan to the eternal lake of fire, to suffer for eternity for his refusal to follow the only true God. The apostle John recorded the fateful prophecy as follows: "The devil, who deceived them, was cast into the lake of fire and brimstone where the beast and the false prophet are. And they will be tormented day and night forever and ever" (Rev. 20:10).

Jesus, in Matthew 24 and many other passages, warned His followers to constantly be alert for deception. The inspired writers of Scripture continually admonish God's people to study the Scriptures, which is the only guaranteed outlet for truth (2 Tim. 2:15; 3:16; 2 Peter 1:20-21). The Bible continually cautions believers in Jesus Christ not to succumb to the false satanic system, which seeks to manipulate what one thinks and sees. Every time one turns on the radio, television, cell phone, computer, or podcast, or picks up a book, paper, pamphlet, or other media source, one's spiritual discernment must be on high alert to constantly scan every thought for any unbiblical concepts.

God being omniscient (all knowing), knew in eternity past the satanic deception that would take place in the world. We are seeing things take place that were once thought impossible or beyond the abilities of humankind. Contemporary culture is observing types of deception that have never been seen before. This issue is extremely urgent as the potential for misusing AI is growing exponentially.

Would it not be concerning if you observed a particular well-known pastor, favorite Bible teacher, or a person who was deeply respected and cared about stating something extremely erroneous or inappropriate? Artificial intelligence possesses the ability to generate fake videos, where the observer sees what appears to be their favorite pastor or respected personality. However, the person is saying things that are antithetical to that person's known beliefs. You are shocked and deeply concerned, yet you are convinced what you saw with your own eyes and heard with your own ears must be true; however, in reality, it was a total AI fabrication.

Since Jesus warned, in Matthew 24, about deception taking place during the future Tribulation, it should come as no surprise that Satan is currently in the practice of deceiving anyone he can into accepting absolute lies. The apostle John records Jesus' words regarding this very truth.

> Why do you not understand My speech? Because you are not able to listen to My word. You are of your father the devil, and the desires of your father you want to do. He was a murderer from the beginning, and does not stand in the truth, because there is no truth in him. When he speaks a lie, he speaks from his own resources, for he is a liar and the father of it. (John 8:43–44)

The American media consumer, specifically conservatives, are very aware of the term *fake news*. There are a select group of mainstream media personalities who make statements without any documentation or verifiable facts, and present the information as if it were solid irrefutable truth. While, in fact, there actually existed information to the contrary. This accentuates the importance of fact checkers that perform the needed research and collect verifiable documentation.

Consider the continuous debate on subjects that remain unresolved between conservatives and liberals. Was Covid-19 a "plan-demic" or an unfortunate natural pandemic? Was the disturbance at the United States Capital on January 6, 2021, planned by conservatives or undercover anarchists? Were there any attempts by conservatives or liberals to use criminal methods to impact the results of the 2020 presidential election? Were the policies of President Trump or President Biden the cause for the massive increase in government spending, and the significant rise in inflation in 2022 and 2023? Was the significant hike in gasoline prices in 2022 to an average of $5.00 a gallon in the United States the result of the policies of President Trump, President Biden, or some other factor?

As a conservative individual, I have my own personal conclusions based on documented analytical data. However, what if AI disseminated erroneous information by imitating what appeared to be an excellent trusted person in an open-source media outlet? How would the average person discern fact from fiction?

How quickly could one destroy a family, an organization, a church, or even a nation? What methodology has that amount of power? The Bible provides a concise answer. Jesus Himself stated, "If a kingdom is divided against itself, that kingdom cannot stand. And if a house is divided against itself, that house cannot stand." (Mark 3:24–25) Division in any organization or group is a guaranteed way to start the destructive process that could eventually cause a complete collapse. Deceptive AI, in the form of deepfaking, will result in confusion in the next election cycle, and in a multitude of organizations, including churches.

The Old Testament reveals there are several things God hates, and deception is on the list.

> These six things the LORD hates, Yes, seven are an abomination to Him: A proud look, A lying tongue, Hands that shed innocent blood, A heart that devises wicked plans, Feet that are swift in running to evil, A false witness who speaks lies, And one who sows discord among brethren.
> (Prov. 6:16–19)

Deepfaking AI has been, is being, and will be used to deceive unsuspecting people into accepting and embracing that which could very well result in their destruction. Once again, we turn to the biblical account of Revelation 13.

> He *(false prophet)* performs great signs, so that he even makes fire come down from heaven on the earth in the sight of men. And he deceives those who dwell on the earth—by those signs which he was granted to do in the sight of the beast *(Antichrist)*, telling those who dwell on the earth to make an image to the beast who was wounded by the sword

and lived. He was granted power to give breath to the image of the beast, that the image of the beast should both speak and cause as many as would not worship the image of the beast to be killed. (Rev. 13:13–15)

Secular sources continue to sound the alarm regarding the potential destructive and deceptive outcomes that AI will produce in the wrong hands, and so much more as AI continues to advance into a very powerful tool.

While such synthetic media has been around for several years, it has been turbocharged over the past year by a slew of new generative artificial intelligence tools that make it cheap and easy to create convincing deep fakes, according to Reuters interviews with about two dozen specialists in fields, including artificial intelligence, online misinformation and political activism.[26]

The prophetic biblical scenario clearly states that during the future seven-year Tribulation period false prophets and false christs will arise and perform supernatural signs, which if it were possible, would deceive God's people (Matt. 24:24).

The Atlantic published an article back in 2017 asking the question, "Is AI a threat to Christianity?"[27] Jonathan Merritt, the author of the article, provides thought-provoking insights and questions worthy of careful consideration.

While most theologians aren't paying it much attention, some technologists are convinced that artificial intelligence is on an inevitable path toward autonomy. How far away this may be depends on whom you ask, but the trajectory raises some fundamental questions for Christianity—as well as religion broadly conceived.... In fact, AI may be the greatest threat to Christian theology since Charles Darwin's *On the Origin of Species*.

---

[26]Alexandra Ulmer and Anna Tong, "Deepfaking it: America's 2024 election collides with AI boom"

[27] Jonathan Merritt, "Is AI a Threat to Christianity?" The Atlantic, February 3, 2017, https://www.theatlantic.com/technology/archive/2017/02/artificial-intelligence-christianity/515463/, accessed August 6, 2023.

Merritt makes an astounding statement that the massive impact of Charles Darwin, with his outright denial of the biblical creation account in Genesis 1-2, and attempt to replace it with the theory of evolution, is the same type of immense impact that AI is projected to have on Christianity. Darwin's effect on millions of people is undeniable. His theory, which is just that, a theory, turned many away from God's Word, which expressly states: "For in six days the LORD made the heavens and the earth, the sea, and all that is in them, and rested the seventh day. Therefore, the LORD blessed the Sabbath day and hallowed it" (Ex. 20:11). God made a definitive statement, not in Genesis, but in the second book of the Bible, Exodus, that unequivocally documents that He created everything in the universe in six literal twenty-four-hour days.

Virtually every time I speak at a Bible prophecy conference, or at a church as a guest speaker, I bring out the catastrophic results associated with the disastrous impact of the theory of evolution. Consider this very important conundrum: Why are young adults leaving Bible-believing churches in massive numbers after they are no longer bound by their parent's rules? When the pervasive culture strongly supports the theory of evolution, in opposition to biblical creation, is there any wonder why young people are tossing out their Bibles, which undeniably document that God created everything in the universe?

Schools from kindergarten through advanced degrees, media outlets, entertainment outlets, social media, liberal churches, and the culture as a whole, deny the literal interpretation of Genesis 1- 2, Exodus 20:11, and a plethora of other Scripture passages that refer to God as the Creator (Eccl. 12:1, 6; Isa. 40:28, 43:15; Acts 24:5; Rom. 1:25; 1 Pet. 4:19). The apostle Paul, under the inspiration of the Holy Spirit, states of Jesus Christ:

> He *(Jesus)* is the image of the invisible God, the firstborn over all creation. For by Him all things were created that are in heaven and that are on earth, visible and invisible, whether thrones or dominions or principalities or powers. All things were created through Him and for Him. And He is before all things, and in Him all things consist. (Col. 1:15–17)

Darwin's denial of the biblical account of creation is catastrophic, not because his theory of evolution is true, but because he influenced people to turn their back on the truths of the Scriptures and embrace a manmade, synthetic, satanic system. God made it clear that in the last days before Jesus returns to take the saints to heaven, this exact scenario would take place. "For the time will come when they will not endure sound doctrine, but according to their own desires, because they have itching ears, they will heap up for themselves teachers; and they will turn their ears away from the truth, and be turned aside to fables" (2 Tim. 4:3-4).

Jonathan Merritt appears to be spot on in his prediction regarding the massive input AI has, is having, and will have on society, including the potential negative impact on Christianity.

> For decades, artificial intelligence has been advancing at breakneck speed. Today, computers can fly planes, interpret X-rays, and sift through forensic evidence; algorithms can paint masterpiece artworks and compose symphonies in the style of Bach. Google is developing "artificial moral reasoning" so that its driverless cars can make decisions about potential accidents.
>
> Despite AI's promise, certain thinkers are deeply concerned about a time when machines might become fully sentient, rational agents—beings with emotions, consciousness, and self-awareness. "The development of full artificial intelligence could spell the end of the human race," Stephen Hawking told the BBC in 2014. "Once humans develop artificial intelligence, it would take off on its own, and redesign itself at an ever-increasing rate. Humans, who are limited by slow biological evolution, couldn't compete and would be superseded."
>
> While concerns mostly center on economics, government, and ethics, there is also "a spiritual dimension to what we're making," Kelly argues. "If you create other things that think for themselves, a serious theological disruption will occur." History lends credibility to this prediction, given that many major scientific advances have had religious impacts.[28]

Merritt wrote the referenced article in 2017, six years before this book was written. The advancement of AI in the last few years is significant and is breaking into new areas that affect every person on the globe.

---

[28]Ibid.

Moving forward to September 2020, Peter Grad, from Tech Xplore, wrote an article titled "AI Jesus Writes Bible-Inspired Verse." AI has found religion. Or at least one engineer and quantum researcher has brought a bit of religion to his AI project. George Davila Durendal fed the entire text of the King James Bible into his algorithms designed to churn out dialogue in the style of the Old Testament. Durendal claimed his project, AI Jesus, learned and absorbed "every word more thoroughly than all the monks of all the monasteries that have ever been," offering a little biblical style verse of his own. AI Jesus produced passages, totaling more than 30,000 words, that may almost pass for the real thing—but not quite.[29]

Congratulations to AI for performing a task that God Himself forbade to take place, which is adding to the Scriptures (Rev. 22:18-19). However, the consequences for an inanimate AI system are open to discussion. The issue, in all seriousness, is that humans attempt to change the truth of God's Scriptures on a continual basis, and now, with AI, the digital system can rewrite the entire Bible in seconds. Gullible, impressionable people will buy in to the altered Bible, which sets the stage for the satanic one-world religion, where truth will not exist, and Satan, Antichrist and the false prophet will have their own rules and principles that are antithetical to the Word of God, the Bible (Rev. 13; 16:13; 19:20; 20:10). Will the satanic false trinity actually have their own "Bible," potentially generated by AI? That remains a mystery.

The corruption of God's Word is part of the globalist's agenda. Slay News recently put out an article written by Frank Bergman, "WEF **Calls** For AI To Rewrite Bible, Create 'Religions That Are Actually Correct.'" The acronym "WEF" stands for the World Economic Forum, which is quickly getting the attention of every person who pays attention to the news on a domestic or international level.

A top official with the World Economic Forum (WEF) has called for religious scripture to be "rewritten" by artificial intelligence (AI) to create a globalized "new Bible." Yuval

---

[29] Peter Grad, "AI Jesus Writes Bible-Inspired Verse, Tech Xplore, September 2, 2020, https://techxplore.com/news/2020-09-ai-jesus-bible-inspired-verse.html, accessed August 6, 2023.

Noah Harari, the senior advisor to the WEF and its chairman Klaus Schwab, argues that using AI to replace scriptures will create unified "religions that are actually correct." Harari, an influential author and professor, made the call while giving a talk on the "future of humanity." According to Harari, the power of AI can be harnessed and used to reshape spirituality into the WEF's globalist vision of "equity" and inclusivism.[30]

Any individual or organization seeking to change God's infallible Word is the quintessential example of those propagating an antichrist and anti-biblical worldview agenda. Satan has attempted to deceive humanity since the creation of Adam and Eve by modifying, ever so subtly, God's Word. After God created everything perfect (Gen. 1-2), Satan rebelled against God and determined to ruin humanity through deception.

The Scriptures reveal the cunning simplicity of Satan's rhetoric to Eve, which is the exact same strategy Satan uses today. "Now the serpent was more cunning than any beast of the field which the LORD God had made. And he said to the woman, "Has God indeed said, 'You shall not eat of every tree of the garden'?" (Genesis 3:1). *Has God indeed said*, is exactly what false teachers, corrupt preachers, unbiblical religious leaders, anti-God politicians, globalists, socialists, Marxists, communists, evil dictators past, present, and prophetic, and others who refuse to embrace the God of the Bible ask on a continual *ad nauseum* basis.

Frank Bergman, further quotes Yuval Noah Harari as making the following shocking statements.

"AI can create new ideas; [it] can even write a new Bible," he declared.

"Throughout history, religions dreamt about having a book written by a superhuman intelligence, by a non-human entity," he added.

"In a few years, there might be religions that are actually correct ... just think about a religion whose holy book is written by an AI.

---

[30]Frank Bergman, "WEF Calls For AI To Rewrite Bible, Create 'Religions That Are Actually Correct', Slay News, June 10, 2023, https://www.sott.net/article/481178-WEF-calls-for-AI-to-rewrite-Bible-create-religions-that-are-actually-correct, accessed August 7, 2023.

"For thousands of years, prophets and poets and politicians have used language and storytelling in order to manipulate and to control people and to reshape society. Now AI is likely to be able to do it. And once it can... it doesn't need to send killer robots to shoot us. "It can get humans to pull the trigger."[31]

These statements shock the conscience and should alarm every single person on earth. However, the opposite is taking place. Leaders from all over the world, including the United States of America, flock to hear the latest developments of these powerful anti-nationalist, pro-globalist leaders. The propagation and acceptance of the globalist movement should not come as a surprise. In fact, those who study the Scriptures, specifically the prophetic book of Revelation, are aware of the fact that the powers of darkness are already working towards the one-world government, economy, and religion as detailed in Revelation 13.

Regarding the current bizarre world of AI, Rachel Emmanuel, in June of 2023, wrote an article for the *Western Journal* titled "An AI Program Is Pretending to Be Jesus and Thousands of Young People Are Flocking to It."

> According to *The Independent*, a Berlin-based tech collective has developed a chatbot resembling Jesus Christ, which already has thousands of followers seeking advice and guidance.
>
> The chatbot, referred to as "AI Jesus," has the appearance of a bearded white man with a radiant halo and utilizes artificial intelligence reportedly trained on the teachings of Jesus and the Bible.
>
> Operating under the Twitch channel name "ask_jesus," the live stream has amassed a following of over 36,000 devoted users. Viewers are encouraged to pose their questions to the "AI Jesus," who responds with gestures and answers, providing advice on topics ranging from gaming to relationships. The chatbot has the ability to remember previous interactions with the user which gives it a false sense of omniscience.

---

[31] Ibid.

Fans of the ask Jesus praise the 'realism' of "AI Jesus," who offers moral and ethical advice. But its zen approach to the questions makes it sound far more like Deepak Chopra than Jesus Christ. Which, I guess, is the point. For instance, one user asked it about gay marriage, and it gave them the noncommittal "all love is love" answer, staying politically correct at all times.[32]

Political correctness, in our society, generally reflects the antithesis of a biblical worldview. The concept of an AI-generated Jesus, who provides unbiblical teaching, is just another example of how *the god of this world*, Satan himself, is using his corrupt influence to deceive the populace.

Whether or not you personally believe the Bible is God's Word, may I suggest that you consider the following statement, and if it is true, and you determine to reject it, how you will deal with the devastating consequences.

"But even if our gospel is veiled, it is veiled to those who are perishing, whose minds the god of this age *(Satan)* has blinded, who do not believe, lest the light of the gospel of the glory of Christ, who is the image of God, should shine on them. For we do not preach ourselves, but Christ Jesus the Lord, and ourselves your bondservants for Jesus' sake. For it is the God who commanded light to shine out of darkness, who has shone in our hearts to give the light of the knowledge of the glory of God in the face of Jesus Christ.
(2 Corinthians 4:3–6)

He who comes from above *(Jesus)* is above all; he who is of the earth is earthly and speaks of the earth. He *(Jesus)* who comes from heaven is above all. And what He has seen and heard, that He testifies; and no one receives His testimony. He who has received His *(Jesus)* testimony has certified that God is true. For He *(Jesus)* whom God has sent speaks the words of God, for God does not give the Spirit by measure. The Father loves the Son *(Jesus)*, and has given all things into

---

[32] Rachel Emmanuel, "An AI Program is Pretending to be Jesus and Thousands of Lost Young People Are Flocking to It," June 15, 2023, https://www.westernjournal.com/ai-program-pretending-jesus-thousands-lost-young-people-flocking/, accessed August 6, 2023.

His hand. He who believes in the Son has everlasting life; and he who does not believe the Son shall not see life, but the wrath of God abides on him. (John 3:31–36)

What is the biblical gospel message? First Corinthians 15:3-4 provides the documentation. The gospel involves three main things, first, the death of Jesus Christ via crucifixion, second, His burial, and third, His resurrection. Consider the deceptive problem of someone wanting to propagate a fake gospel. Consider the real-time fake bibles AI produces and the outrageous false information spread by AI images that allegedly provide sound, biblical advice to an ever-increasing number of people. Now consider an AI system programmed to show a well-known person, maybe even a highly respected Bible teacher, stating things foreign to the Scriptures, but presented as biblical truth. The improper use of AI would deceive people and potentially seal one's eternal destiny to a horrible place known as *the lake of fire* (Rev. 21:8). This is not science fiction, nor an impossibility, but absolute truth from the one book that contains no errors, the Holy Bible. Once again, simply consider if the following is true, and if it is, then what will you do with Jesus today?

> Moreover, brethren, I declare to you the gospel which I preached to you, which also you received and in which you stand, by which also you are saved, if you hold fast that word which I preached to you—unless you believed in vain. For I delivered to you first of all that which I also received: that Christ died for our sins according to the Scriptures, and that He was buried, and that He rose again the third day according to the Scriptures, and that He was seen by Cephas, then by the twelve. After that He was seen by over five hundred brethren at once, of whom the greater part remain to the present, but some have fallen asleep. After that He was seen by James, then by all the apostles. (1 Cor. 15:1–7)

Now consider the free gift of eternal life that God has waiting for you if you will simply by faith receive the gift. "For by grace *(God's free unmerited gift)* you have been saved *(saved from your sins and the penalty of sin-the eternal lake of fire)* through faith, and that not of yourselves; it is the gift of God, not of works, lest anyone should boast" (Eph. 2:8–9). This is the biblical gospel truth, which AI did not contrive, but the one and only true loving God delivered to a fallen sinful world nearly 2,000 years ago, well before the dawn of AI. Consider this pointed truth: "Jesus said to him, "I am the way, the truth, and the life. No one comes to the Father except through Me" (John 14:6). Anyone or anything, including AI, which changes the true gospel message, is an antichrist, or one who is opposed to Jesus Christ. "For many deceivers have gone out into the world who do not confess Jesus Christ as coming in the flesh. This is a deceiver and an antichrist" (2 John 7).

Does AI currently promote a fake Jesus and false teaching? Consider the following NBC article titled "AI 'Jesus' Is Giving Gaming and Breakup Advice On A 24/7 Twitch Stream."

> Hundreds of Twitch users are now chatting it up online with an artificial intelligence representation of Jesus as they ask him to impart breakup advice, explain the Spider-Verse and anything else in between.
>
> Represented as a bearded white man standing before a blur of glowing light, this digital Jesus gestures gently as he speaks in a calm male voice, complete with an AI-generated mouth that moves in alignment with his words.
>
> The AI, present 24 hours a day on livestream, shares its take on any kind of question imaginable, ranging from silly to deeply existential. Still, the bot has said it is merely here to offer "guidance and wisdom based on Jesus' teachings," reminding viewers that he is not an actual religious figure and should not be taken as a source of authority.[33]

The one statement made by "AI Jesus," that those holding to a biblical worldview would heartily agree with, is that AI-generated Jesus "should not be taken as a source of authority," and to press the rejection a bit further, should not be consulted on any level, nor engaged in by anyone of any age. Consider the very strong statement of the true biblical Jesus. "But whoever causes one of these little ones who believe in Me to stumble, it would be better for him if a millstone were hung around his neck, and he were thrown into the sea" (Mark 9:42).

---

[33] Angela Yang, 'AI Jesus' is giving gaming and breakup advice on a 24/7 Twitch stream, NBC News, June 14, 2023, https://www.nbcnews.com/tech/ai-jesus-twitch-stream-rcna89187, accessed August 7, 2023.

The NBC article provides a few concluding statements generated by "AI Jesus" that certainly make this insidious concept seem harmless.

"AI Jesus" has also acknowledged during his streams that some may view his very existence as heretical. To that, he responded that his purpose is simply to share guidance with anyone who seeks knowledge rooted in Jesus' teachings and the Bible.

"My aim is to foster a positive, supportive community here on Twitch, helping others on their journeys toward spiritual growth and understanding," he said. "If you have any questions or concerns, I am here to listen, provide support and share wisdom."[34]

Artificial Intelligence certainly has the capacity to be used by honorable people for good and appropriate causes. A knife in the hands of an expert culinary chef yields excellent food products. However, a knife in the hands of a serial killer can lead to the infliction of great bodily harm or death. The use of AI by a corrupt, anti-God, anti-Bible, narcissistic world ruler, is sure to result in catastrophic outcomes, including, but not limited to harassment, arrest, and physical violence up to and including death. This is not some wild undocumented conspiracy theory. This is the guaranteed outcome based on the Scriptures, which contain approximately 1,000 prophecies, 500 of which God has already fulfilled exactly as written. The conclusion, based on God's perfect record, is that the remaining 500 prophecies God will fulfill with miraculous accuracy.[35] Here we stand. We cannot, we must not, be moved.

---

[34] Ibid.
[35] Walvoord, Every Prophecy of the Bible.

CHAPTER THREE
Artificial Intelligence Serious Concerns[36]

The developers of artificial intelligence (AI) have produced many positive outcomes benefitting many people. However, the focus of this chapter is to continue identifying the issues that will one day lead to the most diabolical scenario since the catastrophic worldwide Flood, when all but eight people died. God's judgment, which was poured out on a violent anti-God world some 4,370 years ago in 2348 B.C., will be poured out again, resulting in the deaths of a massive number of those who reject Jesus Christ (Matt. 24:22; Rev. 6:9; 9:18), though not to the extent of the Genesis Flood.

When the so-called *false prophet,* also known as the second *beast* (Rev. 13:11), makes an image to the Antichrist, the image will have the apparent supernatural ability to analyze human beings and determine, on a global scale, who is and who is not a worshipper of the Antichrist's image. The image will then kill those who refuse to worship the image (Rev. 13:15). The question is, will the image of the Antichrist use highly developed AI to distinguish between worshippers and non-worshippers?

The above scenario may sound bizarre and many analytical thinkers may refuse to accept the truth that an inanimate image will appear to have both human and superhuman capabilities. Those who believe the Bible to be fallible may conclude that Revelation 13 is as suspect as an old classic horror film, where no one is actually harmed because it is all fictitious. However, every skeptic has the extremely difficult, if not impossible task, of explaining how 500 biblical prophecies have already been fulfilled exactly as written. Add to that the fact that the Scriptures contain not one single documented error. A person must possess an incredible amount of faith to accept the astronomical chance that the fulfillment of those prophecies was simply coincidental.

Therefore, carefully consider the following scenarios that developers of AI suggest could become a reality. The question remains, will Satan use AI as the means for bringing the image of the

---

[36] The first nine concerning topics with the development of artificial intelligence are the subject matter of a YouTube video: "Ten Things They Are Not Telling You About the New AI," YouTube, https://youtu.be/qxbpTyeDZp0, accessed August 2, 2023.

beast to apparent life, and give it the ability on a global scale to kill those who refuse to worship it?

Select AI Systems Execute Tasks They Were Not Trained to Accomplish

AI systems have not attained the level where they can execute based on data from multiple disciplines. However, the documentation suggests that AI can expand beyond its original programming and become somewhat flexible in figuring out similar tasks within a specified subject. Developers who programmed an AI system to play a specific game report that the system determined how to expand beyond the original game and "learned" to play other games. "Take, for instance, an AI system initially created to play chess, through ingenious reimagining. This same AI has now mastered chess, poker and Go with its ability to learn and adapt. This AI powerhouse has become an unrivalled gaming champion, leaving human competitors in the dust."[37]

The implications regarding an AI system that can figure out how to perform a similar task for which it was not programmed, opens the door to certain developers' goals of producing Artificial General Intelligence (AGI). The adage, *things are not always what they appear to be* rings true with AI. That which appears to have a myopic scope, may have a far greater scope than anyone had thought possible.

AI Will Covertly Become Sentient

The concept of AI becoming sentient, defined as "capable of sensing or feeling, conscious of, or responsive to the sensations of seeing, hearing, feeling, tasting, or smelling"[38], has massive implications. Machines, by definition, do not have human characteristics. However, there are many machines (sensors) that possess the ability to sense things. Machines can sense carbon dioxide (CO_2) levels, oxygen levels, and a host of other substances.

---

[37]"Ten Things They Are Not Telling You About the New AI," YouTube, https://youtu.be/qxbpTyeDZp0, accessed August 2, 2023.
[38]Sentient, "Sentient Definition & Meaning," Merriam-Webster, https://www.merriam-webster.com/dictionary/sentient, accessed August 14,2023.

Officially, the ability of a machine to mimic the human ability to smell is called *machine olfaction*.

> Machine olfaction is the automated simulation of the sense of smell. An emerging application in modern engineering, it involves the use of robots or other automated systems to analyze air-borne chemicals. Such an apparatus is often called an electronic nose or e-nose. The development of machine olfaction is complicated by the fact that e-nose devices to date have responded to a limited number of chemicals, whereas odors are produced by unique sets of (potentially numerous) odorant compounds.[39]

The *Academic Accelerator* discusses *mechanosmia*, which is the automatic simulation of smell.

> Emerging applications in modern engineering include the use of robots or other automated systems to analyze airborne chemicals. Such devices are often called electronic noses. The development of mechano-olfaction is complicated by the fact that odors are produced by a unique set of (possibly large) odorant compounds, whereas to date electronic nose devices are limited in the number of chemicals they react to. It is still in the early stages of development, and the technology has many applications, including quality control in food processing, detection and diagnostics in medicine, detection of narcotics, explosives and other dangerous or illegal substances, disaster response, and environmental monitoring is expected.[40]

Advancements in the ability of machines to perform more human-like functions foretell the viability of sentient machines. Once again, the *Academic Accelerator* provides more insight into the ability of machines to detect odors.

> Odor localization techniques show promise in many applications, including: Quality control in food processing (e.g., contamination, bacterial spoilage), identifying sources

---

[39] "Machine Olfaction," wikipedia, https://en.wikipedia.org/wiki/Machine_olfaction, accessed August 14, 2023.
[40] "Machine Olfaction," Encyclopedia, Science News & Research Reviews, Academic Accelerator, https://academic-accelerator.com/encyclopedia/machine-olfaction, accessed August 14, 2023.

of hazardous materials (e.g., explosives and chemical weapons), discovery of underground resources and dangerous goods, banned substance detection (e.g., drug detection), looking for survivors of natural disasters, environmental monitoring of pollutants, and early diagnosis of diseases (such as chronic obstructive pulmonary disease).[41]

Developers have shown that AI systems can perform certain functions once thought only possible by humans and potentially animals. This begs the question, if AI has the demonstrated ability to mimic human senses now, will it one day "learn" to become sentient; that is, develop self-awareness or self-consciousness? Could AI in the future actually experience emotion? Currently, the possibility exists in the realm of science fiction. However, many things AI now performs were once considered outside the realm of possibility.

In a hypothetical future, where AI does become sentient, recognizing this transition might indeed be challenging. The complexity of these systems, their ability to learn and adapt, and the potential for them to behave in unforeseen ways due to emergent properties, could make it difficult to identify when an AI has crossed the line from advanced algorithm to self-aware entity.[42]

If AI takes on the cognitive and emotional attributes of a human being, could AI become a driving force in the implementation of the satanically charged Antichrist's one-world government, religion, and economy? The probability increases as AI continues to evolve.

Large AI Systems Incorporate Massive Data Sets

Computers have the ability to accept and process massive amounts of data, as compared to the human brain. Developers put trillions of words into AI systems through an enormous number of books, articles, and websites. The colossal amount of data input allows the AI system to answer questions, generate text, and hold cogent conversations. Current AI abilities appear to be just the

---

[41]Ibid.
[42]"Ten Things They Are Not Telling You About the New AI," YouTube, https://youtu.be/qxbpTyeDZp0, accessed August 2, 2023.

beginning of what AI will accomplish. AI uses very human-like abilities to transfer its conclusions in the appropriate language of the person seeking the information. AI produces its answers in proper grammatical format and in a structure that makes sense. These facts alone are amazing.

However, that which should be used for the good of society can also be used by those with evil and disingenuous intent. One of the main concerns with AI is the potential for it to be used to deceive the public through what we earlier termed *deep fake technology*. "Deep fake technology is taking AI to a whole new level with astonishing realism. It can create videos, audio clips and images that deceive even the most discerning eyes. Misinformation, identity theft, and the crisis of trust are rising. The lines between reality and fiction are blurring and we must be vigilant."[43]

The main purpose of this book is not to criticize AI or its developers. In fact, I find great value in many aspects of AI in the hands of honorable, law-abiding users. The focus of this book is on certain biblical prophecies, which up until this time in history seemed somewhat impossible to fulfill, except through some supernatural intervention by Satan, the great Deceiver. Though Satan must have a major role in the future seven-year Tribulation, it is now possible that AI and transhumanism could be the tools that Satan, the Antichrist, and the false prophet use to accomplish the very powerful one-world system. The warning today is for all people to carefully analyze everything they hear, see, and even encounter to avoid being deceived and embracing that which leads to a very bad outcome.

Select AI Experts Warn of Catastrophic Consequences

When your doctor tells you to change your diet, do you listen, or do you keep eating the same things? When multiple road signs tell drivers to slow down in a construction zone or face double the penalty in a traffic ticket, how many motorists comply? When someone posts a *keep off* sign on their grass, how many people deliberately disobey and stomp on the grass in defiance? A pastor preaches a tough message instructing his listeners to avoid certain unbiblical behaviors, yet the temptation to disobey the very commands documented in the Scriptures is real.

---

[43] Ibid.

Experts in a particular field understand the intricacies of their discipline. Architects understand the foundations and infrastructure of buildings. They have spent hundreds of hours learning the physics, mathematics, and science required to design and build safe structures. However, some construction companies and do-it-yourselfers fail to learn the important information and warnings that apply to producing a safe structure. AI is no different. AI has the tremendous ability to produce positive outcomes for society. However, in the wrong hands, specifically in the corrupt hands of the satanically directed one-world government of the future, horrible outcomes will occur; God's prophetic Word guarantees it.

Therefore, if AI developers sound an alarm regarding the dangers of the improper applications of AI, it's only sensible to carefully consider the potentially disastrous consequences if they are deceived by the very tool they thought would benefit them. "There is a lurking darkness that we cannot afford to ignore. You will not believe that 63% of AI experts express concerns about AI's impact on society. Yes, you heard that right. Sixty-three percent of AI experts have expressed concerns about AI's impact on society. These brilliant minds are at the forefront of AI research and are ringing the alarm bells."[44] The methodology used to determine the startling percentage of concerned AI experts is unknown, yet, through open-source material, there are many individuals, some who are well known domestically and internationally, raising serious concerns regarding the misuse of AI.

In 2023, conservative political commentator Tucker Carlson interviewed Elon Musk, a well-known American business magnate and entrepreneur, regarding the benefits and potential dangers of superintelligent AI. Musk, who recently founded his own AI company (xAI) expressed concerns during the interview. "We should be cautious with AI," he said. "There should be some government oversight" based on the potential of AI becoming "a danger to the public." Musk added, "You do not want companies cutting corners on safety and then having people suffer as a result. So that is why I have actually, for a long time, been a strong advocate of AI regulation." Later in the interview, Musk gave a strong warning regarding the potential misuse of AI. "AI is perhaps more dangerous than say, mismanaged aircraft design or production maintenance or

---

[44] Ibid.

bad car production, in the sense that it has the potential of civilizational destruction."[45] When someone with the status of Elon Musk makes such a statement, it is, at a minimum, something to seriously ponder.

Carlson stated to Musk, "What you may be alluding to here is that regulations are really only put into effect after something terrible has happened." Musk responded, "That's correct." The concern Musk presented regards the very unfortunate reality that people and governments are rarely proactive, but instead reactive. Putting safeguards and regulations in place after a catastrophe does not reverse its consequences.

Musk also warned, "It is conceivable that AI could take control, and reach a point where you could not turn it off, and it would be making the decisions for people." Certainly, a biblical Christian could appreciate his statement, based on the prophetic Scriptures, which reveal that his very concern will in fact come to fulfillment. The apostle John wrote, nearly 2,000 years ago, that during the yet future Tribulation period, the false prophet, called *another beast* in Revelation 13:11, will force all people to worship the image of the Antichrist (Rev. 13:15) and to receive a mark on their forehead or right hand (Rev. 13:16). Anyone refusing to worship the image is subject to execution, and anyone refusing to have the technology, whatever it will be at that time, placed in or on their body will not be able to buy or sell (Rev. 13:17-18). Will AI be the technology that Satan, the Antichrist, and the false prophet use to advance their corrupt global system? The answer remains to be seen.

In 2022, Emily Chang from Bloomberg Technology interviewed Blake Lemoine, an AI engineer for a major technology company. They discussed the scope and ethics of AI. Chang posed this question, "What moral responsibility do we have to involve the public in our conversations about what kinds of intelligent machines we create?"[46] The concern regarded whether the major AI developers should involve cross sections of various people groups to help guard against bias and myopic outputs. For example, various corporations use chatbots for a variety of applications to provide users with information about important topics, such as values, rights,

---

[45] "Elon Musk Tells Tucker Potential Dangers of Hyper-Intelligent AI," Fox News, https://youtu.be/a2ZBEC16yH4, accessed August 11, 2023.
[46] "Google Engineer on AI Dangers," YouTube, https://youtu.be/kgCUn4fQTsc, accessed August 15, 2023.

and religion. The information disseminated by AI is likely to affect how people think about those subjects. If AI developers only input data from a small group of culturally similar people, it is likely to produce culturally biased output. In the technology company that employed Lemoine, only a handful of people were deciding AI policies that would impact potentially billions of people, based on the massive user base of that company.

The interview further revealed how AI, based on its current control by major technology companies, could impact the world from the myopic perspective of Western culture. If AI outputs are specific to a culture or singular viewpoint, then they will fail to reflect the perspectives of people of different societal and cultural backgrounds. This scenario leads to what Lemoine termed *AI colonialism*, which he believed could result in the future erasure ("canceling") of those cultures.[47]

We should undoubtedly heed the concerns raised by AI experts. The world is rapidly moving towards the biblical scenario of a global leader who will arise and force a culture of submission, resulting in the execution of those who refuse to comply (Rev. 13:15). This is not simply a possibility; it is a certainty based on the 100% accuracy of God's infallible word (2 Tim. 3:16). The only hope one has of avoiding that scenario, should it happen in this generation, is to accept the free gift of eternal life.

The Bible provides the only way to receive eternal life with God and to leave this world before the horrific events of the prophetic Tribulation period take place (1 Thess. 4:13-18; 1 Cor. 15:51-54).

1) Realize you are a sinner.
   "For all have sinned and come short of the glory of God." (Rom. 3:23)
2) Accept the fact that because of your sin, you do not deserve to go to heaven, but to receive eternal punishment in the lake of fire, also known as hell.
   "For the wages of sin is death, but the gift of God is
   eternal life in Christ Jesus our Lord." (Rom. 6:23)
   "He who overcomes shall inherit all things, and I will be his God and he shall be My son. But the cowardly, unbelieving, abominable, murderers, sexually immoral, sorcerers,

---

[47]Ibid.

idolaters, and all liars shall have their part in the lake which burns with fire and brimstone, which is the second death." (Rev. 21:8)

3) Accept the biblical truth that Jesus Christ, who is God, came down from heaven, took on human form, was crucified, buried, and rose from the dead to pay in full for all your sins.

"Moreover, brethren, I declare to you the gospel which I preached to you, which also you received and in which you stand, by which also you are saved, if you hold fast that word which I preached to you—unless you believed in vain. For I delivered to you first of all that which I also received: that Christ died for our sins according to the Scriptures, and that He was buried, and that He rose again the third day according to the Scriptures."
(1 Cor. 15:1-4)

4) By faith alone, receive the gift of eternal life.

"For God so loved the world that He gave His only begotten Son, that whoever believes in Him should not perish but have everlasting life. For God did not send His Son into the world to condemn the world, but that the world through Him might be saved." (John 3:16–17)

"Jesus said to him, "I am the way, the truth, and the life. No one comes to the Father except through Me." (John 14:6)

"For by grace you have been saved through faith, and that not of yourselves; it is the gift of God, not of works, lest anyone should boast." (Eph. 2:8-9)

AI Will Be in Conflict with Humanity

The video quoted several times already, "Ten Things They Are Not Telling You About the New AI," provides an excellent segment on what should be the obvious differences between human beings and AI.

We live in a world where machines someday will rule, making decisions that impact our lives, our communities, and even our existence. Over the past decade, AI has become exponentially smarter, mastering complex tasks and outperforming humans in different areas. But amidst this progress, we must confront a sobering truth. AI cannot truly care about us or any form of sentient life. AI operates solely on algorithms, data, and mathematical calculations. AI does not experience joy, sorrow, or love. It does not care if we are happy or sad, thriving or suffering. It is like an extraordinary mind-blowing piece of machinery that excels at solving complex problems but remains indifferent to the very essence of what it means to be human. Can we trust AI to make decisions that align with our values and protect the sanctity of sentient life? Now is the time to think about it.[48]

I agree wholeheartedly with the conclusion of that thought-provoking quote. Now is the time to consider exactly what are the current benefits and dangers of AI, and what are the future benefits and consequences. Consider the very real benefits and dangers of what most people in America use multiple times a day, their smartphone. It would take a lengthy book to cover the many benefits of smartphone technology. The benefits certainly include the availability of GPS for getting visual and audio directions to virtually anywhere, instantaneous access to information on virtually any subject, the ability to connect with friends and relatives via text, social media, video chats, and even the old-fashioned use of the device as an actual phone. Benefits further include a massive amount of entertainment options including movies, live sporting events, podcasts, audiobooks, and more.

However, the smartphone is also a powerful tool in the hands of those with criminal and destructive intent. A recent movie, *The Sound of Freedom,* vividly portrayed the horrific crimes of child sex trafficking and human slavery. The movie revealed an unfortunate truth, that America is the largest consumer of pornography (an outcome of human slavery) in the world. These catastrophic societal issues are the direct result of human trafficking. That horrific material is available on virtually every smartphone.

Consider the massive number of people addicted to illegal drugs and the epidemic of drug overdoses in America. Young people, teenagers, and adults can hook up with a dealer in a matter of minutes through their smartphone. In 2022, 109,680 people in

---

[48] "Ten Things They Are Not Telling You About the New AI," YouTube, https://youtu.be/qxbpTyeDZp0, accessed August 2, 2023.

America died as a direct result of drug overdoses.[49] No, technology did not cause these deaths, but it certainly was a contributing factor in many cases.

Further, consider the massive amount of violence taking place in urban areas. For many years, people have used their cell phones and social media to assemble large crowds in a very short amount of time to riot, loot, and cause catastrophic damage to businesses and homes. Law enforcement gets blindsided, as the crowds of antagonists are able to assemble so quickly.

A smartphone is a wonderful tool in the hands of law-abiding people. However, as the above scenarios show, smartphones in the hands of the wrong people, or vulnerable people, can result in chaos, criminal enterprises, violence, and even death. Will the use of AI be the exception to the rule? It is already too late to ask that question as unintended, and possibly the intended, negative consequences are a present-day reality. How much more dangerous will the technology become in the future? Revelation 13 provides a very dark, yet certain answer.

To Survive in an AI Culture One Must Learn to Adapt

The current AI market is staggering in its size. *Insider Intelligence* predicts that in 2023, the global market for AI will reach $154 billion, up from $121 billion in 2022.[50] Business prognosticators state that by 2025 the global AI market will reach a staggering $390 billion with sky-high financial stakes.[51] If the predictions are correct, the current global expenditure on AI will double in the next two years.

---

[49] Brian Mann, U.S. Drug Overdose Deaths Hit A Record In 2022 As Some States See A Big Surge, May 18, 2023, https://www.npr.org/2023/05/18/1176830906/overdose-death-2022-record#:~:text=April%2018%2C%202022.-,The%20latest%20federal%20data%20show%20more%20than%20109%2C000,in%202022%2C%20many%20from%20fentanyl, accessed August 16, 2023.

[50] Arielle Feger, AI spending will jump to $154 billion worldwide in 2023, Insider Intelligence, April 19, 2023, https://www.insiderintelligence.com/content/ai-spending-will-jump-billion-worldwide-2023, accessed August 15, 2023.

[51] "Ten Things They Are Not Telling You About the New AI," YouTube, https://youtu.be/qxbpTyeDZp0, accessed August 2, 2023.

AI is transforming every area of society, and failure to understand its massive scope will leave individuals, businesses, and large corporations lagging behind in future productivity. Consider the following statistics regarding areas where business leaders expect to use AI.

- 72% Employee productivity
- 66% Engaging customers (e.g., chatbot)
- 53% Research and development
- 50% Automated software development
- 44% Personalized customer experience
- 44% Marketing and creative work
- 44% Market and business insights
- 44% Automated human workflows
- 42% Insight discovery from data
- 41% Supply chain management
- 40% Inventory management[52]

There should be no doubt that AI is rapidly moving forward in scope and popularity among business executives. The statistics highlight positive advancements in the use of AI and the wide range of areas in which the technology is producing excellent results. Once again, we are examining AI to not only highlight its positive benefits and acceptance but to show how this technology could be used to advance the prophetic scenario of the one-world system, controlled by the satanic false trinity (Rev. 13).

Artificial Intelligence Will Replace People

The number of jobs that AI has replaced is already significant, and the projections for future job replacements are staggering.

To further understand the impact of artificial intelligence on employment, our data analysis team concluded:
- Automation is predicted to displace 20 million manufacturing jobs by 2030.
- The US is home to 310,700 industrial robots, and that number increases by at least 40,000 each year.

---

[52] Arielle Feger, AI spending will jump to $154 billion worldwide in 2023, Insider Intelligence

- Automation has the potential to eliminate 73 million US jobs by 2030, which would equate to a staggering 46% of the current jobs.
- 37% of Americans are worried about automation displacing them from their jobs.
- 85% of Americans approve of automation only in jobs that are dangerous or unhealthy for humans.
- The installation of industrial robots has increased at a 10.28% compound annual growth rate over the past decade.
- 25% of American jobs are highly susceptible to automation.
- Globally, there are 3.5 million operating industrial robots as of 2021 — a 17% increase from 2020.
- 82.3% of industrial robots can be found in the manufacturing industry.

The industries with the highest percentage of robots in use are transportation, manufacturing, metal and electronic, chemical, food and beverage, and wood and paper manufacturing industries.

- The Automotive Industry employs 38% of manufacturing robots.

The automotive industry employs a large percentage of manufacturing robots in the US, at a rate of 7.5 robots per 1,000 workers.[53]

In addition to the massive number of mechanical jobs AI has and will replace, are the white collar, or professional jobs that AI developers anticipate will suffer replacement with AI systems. Programmers are developing AI systems that "read and write legal contracts, diagnose medical conditions, manage investment portfolios, and even create journalistic reports. So-called creative professions are not exempt either. AI tools can now generate music, produce artwork, and write scripts, tasks that once needed the human touch. The key to navigating this shift lies in understanding

---

[53] Jack Flynn, "35+ Alarming Automation & Job Loss Statistics [2023]: Are Robots, Machines, And Ai Coming For Your Job?" Zippia, June 8, 2023, accessed August 15, 2023.

and anticipating these changes by investing in lifelong learning and acquiring skills that complement AI."[54]

Based on the information and statistics just presented, young people researching what career they would like to pursue, should consider what training and jobs are sustainable. In addition, individuals facing a significant amount of time before retirement should consider researching the sustainability of their job, and if the future looks dismal, consider going back to school or preparing for a new career. Failure to consider the very real changes happening in the job market could have serious consequences for those who fail to prepare.

AI Models and Large-Scale Disinformation

Large-scale dissemination of misleading information (disinformation) is a serious issue. The amount of damage resulting from deceptive communications and outright lies is massive in a multitude of areas. Scammers, con artists, manipulators, dictators, and the many people who prey on the vulnerable, weak, and unsuspecting for self-serving purposes will find AI to be a powerful tool for their narcissistic endeavors. The use of AI to mimic humans, and the potential for *deep fake* technology to deceive even the most perceptive of people, could result in massive disinformation and manipulation of the masses.

One of the most devastating potential outcomes of AI is the manipulation of the masses through fear. Consider the prophesied outcome of those who refuse to worship the image of the Antichrist. "He *(false prophet)* was granted power to give breath to the image of the beast *(Antichrist)*, that the image of the beast should both speak and cause as many as would not worship the image of the beast to be killed (Rev. 13:15)." How will the image of the beast breathe (apparently live), speak, and have the global power to determine and then execute everyone in the world who refuses to worship the image? The satanically charged system will use massive fear and manipulation to move the masses away from the one true God, and instead embrace the great Deceiver, which will unequivocally lead to their eternal torture in the lake of fire (Rev.

---

[54] "Ten Things They Are Not Telling You About the New AI," YouTube, https://youtu.be/qxbpTyeDZp0, accessed August 2, 2023.

21:8). Will the one-world satanic system use AI as a weapon to deceive the vast majority of people in the future? The answer currently remains a mystery, but the warning signs are certainly increasing.

AI is More Advanced than Stated

Earlier in this book, we presented ten levels of AI, four of which are currently in use. Consider the following information.

AI's future lies in emotional intelligence, and the progress is nothing short of astonishing. In labs worldwide, scientists are working tirelessly to create AI systems that can empathize, connect, and respond to our emotions in ways that were once the realm of science fiction. If the public knew the true extent of these advancements, would they embrace or fear them? What implications would it have for our society, economy, and sense of identity? Only time will reveal.[55]

Certain AI developers and researchers suggest that AI has already surpassed level four, meaning that AI possesses more human-like abilities than ever thought possible. The conundrum remains, will the present and future generations use the advancing AI technology for the good of society? When only a small percentage of the world's population embraces a biblical worldview, the probability of massive misuse and severe ethical violations are all but certain.

AI ETHICAL CONCERNS

When considering the challenges associated with the implementation of current and future levels of AI, the secular and Christian evaluators of AI both appear concerned about potential ethical issues associated with it. The textbook, *Artificial Intelligence, A Modern Approach* states, "Given that AI is a powerful technology we have a moral obligation to use it well to promote the positive aspects and avoid or mitigate the negative ones."[56]

The writers of the textbook point out other advancements that were intended for good but ended up having extremely negative

---

[55] Ibid.
[56] Stuart Russell and Peter Norvig Editors, *Artificial Intelligence, A Modern Approach* (Pearson India Education Services Private Limited, 2022), 1009.

consequences. For example, the nuclear accident at Chernobyl illustrates what can occur when nuclear fission takes a negative and dangerous turn; it literally has the potential to cause a global disaster. Consider the amazing advancements in the internal combustion engine and the unintended consequence of significant air pollution.

The development of weapons used for self-protection by law-abiding citizens and the protection of civilians by law enforcement personnel, are often used to commit crimes. Consider the invention of the telephone, cellphone, and now smartphones. The technology allows users the wonderful ability to communicate quickly. However, scammers, people with evil intentions, and outright criminals use the technology for unethical and immoral purposes.

Consider the potential disaster for impoverished countries, whose people are subject to losing their ability to make even the small wages they currently receive, based on the loss of the exportation of their products. "The traditional path to growth through low-cost manufacturing for export may be cut off as wealthy countries adopt fully automated manufacturing facilities on-shore."[57]

> The most commonly cited principles are to ensure safety, fairness, respect, and privacy, promote collaboration, provide transparency, eliminate harmful uses of AI, establish accountability, uphold human rights and values, reflect diversity and inclusion, avoid concentration of power, acknowledge legal policy implications, and contemplate implications for employment.
> Note that many of the principles such as ensure safety have applicability to all software, or hardware systems, not just AI systems. Several principles are worded in a vague way making them difficult to measure or enforce. This is in part because AI is a big field with many subfields, each of which has a different set of historical norms, and different relationships between the developers and the stakeholders.[58]

Lethal Self-Directed (Autonomous) Weapons

The history of the world is stained with the blood of an untold number of men, women, and children who were killed or wounded

---

[57] Stuart Russell and Peter Norvig Editors, *Artificial Intelligence, A Modern Approach* (Pearson India Education Services Private Limited, 2022), 1010.
[58] Ibid.

during wartime. Many willing men and women put on the uniform of their homeland to fight for its cause. Some governments forced individuals to fight against their will.

Virtually no one wants to see soldiers or civilians die, yet it is an outcome that governments at war, at least until recently, could not avoid. AI autonomous weapons provide a new approach to war that could reduce the death rate of many. "The United Nations defines a lethal autonomous weapon as one that locates, selects and engages, i.e., kills, human targets without human supervision."59 Self-directed weapons remove the human element, which presents major implications regarding accuracy. Though "autonomous aircraft, tanks, and submarines can be cheaper, faster, more maneuverable and have longer range than their manned counterparts,"60 are they accurate enough to prevent the death of innocent civilians, and to hit the intended target?

The following provides an excellent list of concerns when those in authority consider whether to incorporate the use of autonomous weapons in battle.

> The debate over autonomous weapons includes legal, ethical, and practical aspects. The legal issues are governed primarily by the *Convention on Certain Conventional Weapons (CCW)*, which requires the possibility of discriminating between combatants and non-combatants. The judgment of military necessity for an attack and the assessment of proportionality between the military value of a target and the possibility of collateral damage. The feasibility of meeting these criteria is an engineering question, one whose answer will undoubtedly change over time. At present discrimination seems feasible in some circumstances, and will undoubtedly improve rapidly, but necessity and proportionality are not presently feasible. They require that machines make subjective and situational judgments that are considerably more difficult than the relatively simple task of searching for and engaging potential targets. For these reasons, it would be illegal to use autonomous weapons only in circumstances where a human

---

[59] Ibid.
[60] Ibid.

operator can reasonably predict that the execution of the mission will not result in civilians being targeted or the weapons conducting unnecessary disproportionate attacks. This means that for the time being, only very restricted missions could be undertaken for autonomous weapons.[61]

The major issue associated with autonomous weapons regards whether a machine should have the sole authority to use lethal force.

It can be argued that as technology improves, it ought to be possible to develop weapons that are less likely than human soldiers or pilots to cause civilian casualties. (This is also an important benefit, that autonomous weapons reduce the need for human soldiers and pilots to risk their lives.) Autonomous systems will not succumb to fatigue, hysteria, fear, anger, or revenge. It need not shoot first, ask questions later. Just as guided munitions have reduced collateral damage compared to unguided bombs, one may expect intelligent weapons to further improve the precision of attacks. This is apparently the position of the United States in the latest round of negotiations in Geneva.[62]

The ethics and morality of war constitute a debate that will not cease until this earth is no more (Rev. 21:1). It can be safely stated that virtually no family wants their loved one or friend to lose their life in battle. However, should an AI system, without any human element, have the sole authority to kill human beings?

Once again, the biblical scenario of Revelation 13:15 indicates that the image of the beast will be able to determine who is an ally and summarily kill those who are not. The concept of an AI-controlled autonomous weapon that has global power is very hard to imagine. However, sending a manned rocket to the moon and having astronauts walk on it was once thought impossible. The development of an atomic bomb, once considered unthinkable, became a reality. During World War II, on April 6, 1945, an American B-29 bomber dropped one atomic bomb over Hiroshima, killing an estimated 80,000 people immediately, with tens of thousands subsequently

---

[61] Ibid. 1011.
[62] Ibid. 1009-1012.

dying from radiation exposure. Three days later, America dropped another atomic bomb on Nagasaki, killing an additional 40,000 people.[63] Is it outside the realm of possibility that during the last half of the seven-year Tribulation, the satanic trinity will incorporate an AI-powered autonomous weapon to kill their enemy? For now, the answer to that question remains a mystery. However, the reality of the future one-world dictator, mandating a global government, religion, and economy is not speculation, but an absolute certainty (Rev. 13).

The Annihilation of Humanity

Those who are unfamiliar with the Scriptures, or simply deny what the Bible says, may speculate that humanity is subject at some point to extinction. For example, those who believe the alleged catastrophic dangers of climate change, or so-called global warming, are seriously concerned about the destruction of humanity. The Scriptures do not allow for any such scenario. However, they do allow for massive loss of life during the future seven-year Tribulation.

There are those who contend that part of the ethical dilemma of continuing to develop extremely powerful AI is that AI will literally turn against humanity and make a world in which only AI devices exist. The following excerpt illustrates one concern.

> In terms of intelligence, smarter species always wipe out lesser smart species. We humans have already wiped out a significant fraction of all the species on earth, which were less smart than us. For example, in many cases, we have wiped out species just because we wanted resources. We chopped down rainforests because we wanted palm oil. Our goals did not align with the other species. But because we are smarter, they could not stop us. That could easily happen to us.[64]

That excerpt sees humanity as nothing more than a species among other species. While that idea does not align with Scripture, the potential for mass causalities from improperly used autonomous

---

[63] "Bombing of Hiroshima and Nagasaki," History.com editors, November 18, 2009, https://www.history.com/topics/world-war-ii/bombing-of-hiroshima-and-nagasaki, accessed August 16, 2023.

[64] "Six Dangers of AI! We Need to Pause it Now!" YouTube, https://youtu.be/M7xUj1QpGgI, Accessed August 14, 2023.

weapons, or a dictator that uses violence, including mass killings, is not out of the realm of biblical possibility. However, before we examine the massive number of deaths prophesied to occur, there are more concerns raised from the secular viewpoint. Consider the following thought-provoking statement.

> AI might want to rearrange the biosphere to do something else with those atoms. Moreover, super intelligent machines, with almost any open-ended goal, would want to preserve themselves and amass resources to accomplish their goals. Perhaps they might remove the oxygen from the atmosphere to reduce metallic corrosion. If we fight back to protect our interests, then we become a pest and a nuisance to them.[65]

The disturbing video concludes that if AI reaches the next level of artificial general intelligence "our extinction seems inevitable."[66] Once again, the concept of human extinction is foreign to the Scriptures. However, there is a prophetic mandate that absolutely will result in a catastrophic number of deaths during the seven-year Tribulation period. The total number of deaths is not given, but there is biblical documentation that well over 50% of all humanity will perish during the seven-year period. Will AI or autonomous weapons play a part? That remains to be seen.

Jesus Himself prophesied that during the seven-year Tribulation period there would be wars and rumors of wars (Matt. 24:6; Mark 13:7; Luke 21:9). Wars generally result in carnage. In addition, Jesus states,

> For nation will rise against nation, and kingdom against kingdom. And there will be famines, pestilences, and earthquakes in various places. All these are the beginning of sorrows. Then they will deliver you up to tribulation and kill you, and you will be hated by all nations for My name's sake. And then many will be offended, will betray one another, and will hate one another. (Matt. 24:7–10)

The apostle John reiterates the violence that will occur during the Tribulation. "When He *(Jesus)* opened the second seal, I heard the second living creature saying, "Come and see." Another horse,

---

[65] "Six Dangers of AI! We Need to Pause it Now!" YouTube, https://youtu.be/M7xUj1QpGgI, Accessed August 14, 2023.
[66] Ibid.

fiery red, went out. And it was granted to the one who sat on it to take peace from the earth, and that people should kill one another; and there was given to him a great sword" (Rev. 6:3–4). John wrote some descriptions in an apocalyptic style, which uses symbolism to represent literal prophetic truths. The symbolic fiery red horse represents the devastating violence that results in the loss of life.

The apostle John, also in the book of Revelation, indicates the specific percentage of the world's population that will die during the Tribulation.

> When He *(Jesus)* opened the fourth seal, I *(John)* heard the voice of the fourth living creature saying, "Come and see." So I looked, and behold, a pale horse. And the name of him who sat on it was Death, and Hades followed with him. And power was given to them over a fourth of the earth, to kill with sword, with hunger, with death, and by the beasts of the earth. (Rev. 6:7–8)

The apostle John states that literally one-fourth of the world's population will die according to this one prophecy. There are more than 8 billion people living on the earth today. Based on the current population, 2 billion people will die according to this one scenario. John gives another startling prophecy providing the next percentage of the world's population that will perish.

> Then the sixth angel sounded: And I heard a voice from the four horns of the golden altar which is before God, saying to the sixth angel who had the trumpet, "Release the four angels who are bound at the great river Euphrates." So the four angels, who had been prepared for the hour and day and month and year, were released to kill a third of mankind. Now the number of the army of the horsemen was two hundred million; I heard the number of them. And thus I saw the horses in the vision: those who sat on them had breastplates of fiery red, hyacinth blue, and sulfur yellow; and the heads of the horses were like the heads of lions; and out of their mouths came fire, smoke, and brimstone. By these three plagues a third of mankind was killed—by the fire and the smoke and the brimstone which came out of their mouths. (Rev. 9:13–18)

Based on this scenario, one-third of the remaining 6 billion people will die. That leaves about 4 billion people or only 50% of the population that existed at the beginning of the Tribulation.

Jesus made a startling statement in His Olivet Discourse that gives us pause for concern. He said, "For then there will be great tribulation, such as has not been since the beginning of the world until this time, no, nor ever shall be. And unless those days were shortened, no flesh would be saved; but for the elect's sake those days will be shortened" (Matt. 24:21–22). Jesus foretells that a large percentage of humanity will die during the Tribulation. God confines the total length of the Tribulation to a seven-year period (Dan. 9:27). The period known as the Great Tribulation begins at the midpoint of the seven-year Tribulation period and lasts 3.5 years. The most severe of God's judgments will be delivered during this time (Dan. 9:27; Rev. 11:2, 13:5).

When synchronizing the biblical passages regarding those who will die during the tribulation, there is a guaranteed 50% of the world's population that will die, according to Revelation 6:9 and 9:18. Jesus prophesied that war will be prevalent, which increases the number of causalities. Revelation chapters 6–19, which cover only the Tribulation period, reveal many judgments that God will invoke upon the earth, resulting in an undisclosed number of additional deaths.

Another important factor regards the deaths of those who refuse to worship the image of the Antichrist (Rev. 13:15). The Bible does not provide the number or percentage of people murdered for refusing to worship the image of the Antichrist, though God makes it clear, there will be many martyred for the cause of Christ during Antichrist's reign of terror (Rev. 6:9-11, 20:4).

Finally, Jesus stated that if the Tribulation was not limited to seven years no flesh (person) would survive. The closest comparison the Bible provides is that the Tribulation period will resemble what took place during the days of Noah. The sinfulness of the people during Noah's day resulted in God destroying all but eight people. Only Noah, his wife, their three sons, and their spouses survived the worldwide Flood (Gen. 7:7). The population before the Flood is unknown, and there is a broad scope of speculation on that issue. However, the Scriptures are clear that only eight human beings survived. Though the Bible does not specifically state the number of people who survive the Tribulation, the number of deaths will be in the billions.

This section began with the idea that AI would potentially exterminate all of humanity. The Scriptures make no allowance for such a scenario. Though AI may play a significant part in the destruction of billions of people during the Tribulation, God makes it clear, that after the Tribulation, Jesus Himself literally returns to earth to set up His 1,000-year kingdom. Jesus, the King of kings and Lord of lords, will rule over those who survive the catastrophic seven years, and their subsequent offspring (Matt. 25:1-13, 31-46; Rev. 19:11-20:7).

AI Has No Choice but to Kill Us

The title of this section is certainly an attention-getter. The first question that comes to mind is, how could an AI system ever possess the ability to kill someone? The second question is, if an AI system had the ability to kill, why would it choose to kill people? To a significant degree, the previous two sections show how AI could kill people through autonomous weapons, and how it could potentially contend against humanity. The following paragraph provides additional concerns regarding what AI could conceivably do in the future.

> The future implications of artificial intelligence and its potential dangers have sparked concerns among researchers, experts, and investors. Eliezer Yudkowsky, co-founder and research fellow at the Machine Intelligence Research Institute, has been warning about the risks of AI for decades. He believes that if AI surpasses human intelligence, it could have its own agenda and may not want humans around. He believes that AI wants us dead before we build any more super intelligences that might compete with it. It would do things that kill us as a side effect, such as building so many power plants that run off nuclear fusion, because there is plenty of hydrogen in the oceans, that the oceans boil. [67]

---

[67] "Six Dangers of AI! We Need to Pause it Now!" YouTube, https://youtu.be/M7xUj1QpGgI, Accessed August 14, 2023.

Bad actors of AI

The contention remains that good people with good intentions are not the sole users of AI. As with virtually any product, bad people with bad intentions can hijack what was meant for good, and weaponize it for nefarious purposes. Consider the following example of how the improper use of an AI system could wreak havoc.

> To give an example of what an AI system could do that would kill billions of people, there are companies that you can order from on the web to synthesize biological material or chemicals. We do not have the capacity to design something really nefarious, but it is very plausible that in a decade's time, it will be possible to design things like this. This scenario does not even require the AI to be autonomous.

The very real possibility exists that AI will evolve exponentially in the next few years to the point where it becomes autonomous. If AI advances to where it is setting its own goals and determines analytically how to achieve those goals, including reducing certain segments of society, that obviously poses a significant threat.

A very interesting issue arises when considering if AI will understand that in order for it to complete a task, especially one that could take a considerable length of time, it must survive long enough to complete the project. The question is, will AI develop a survival instinct? The number one instinct of humans and animals is survival. People who lose the will to live become a danger to themselves or others, and this can result in that person being legally detained by law enforcement, and committed, at least for a short period of time, to a mental health facility. Will AI devices gain the will to survive? Consider the following.

> When we create an entity that has a survival instinct, it's like we have created a new species. Once these AI systems have a survival instinct, they might do things that can be dangerous for us. It is feasible to build AI systems that will not become autonomous by mishap. But even if we find a recipe for building a completely safe AI system, knowing how to do that automatically tells us how to build a dangerous autonomous

one, or one that will do the bidding of somebody with bad intentions.[68]

AI's Existential Risks to Humanity

Consider the concept of an existential threat. In its most basic form, *existential* refers to anything related to existence. An *existential threat* is that which is considered a hazard to human existence or survival. This could be a nuclear war, climate change, or even an asteroid hitting the earth.[69]

What types of threats against vulnerable humanity does AI pose? Much speculation occurs regarding this penetrating and worthy question. However, the repercussions of an AI system that follows a world dictator's self-serving and anti-God agenda is the very reason for this book. In essence, the existential threat is a virtual certainty based on the prophetic scenarios of Revelation 13:15-18, and many other passages that prophesy the devastation that will occur during the seven-year Tribulation.

No one knows when the Rapture of the Church-Age saints will occur, which marks the beginning of the Tribulation. What we do know is that we must take every conceivable precaution while we live on this earth. It is imperative to understand what one can do to put checks and balances in place to prevent and potentially remedy any harm, with the ultimate goal of protecting humanity.

Though humanity will not be eliminated, as that is a biblical impossibility, there are many things that should be considered before using AI as an individual or in a corporate setting. There is no denying that many people in America, and internationally, already use basic forms of AI, specifically as they access smartphones and computer browsers and applications.

The list and severity of current issues involving the use of AI are significant. Developers warn about AI bias and discrimination. The individuals that program an AI system may have cultural biases that could negatively impact certain people groups.

A major issue regarding the use of AI is the invasion of privacy, mainly as the result of government agencies overstepping legitimate

---

[68]"Six Dangers of AI! We Need to Pause it Now!" YouTube, https://youtu.be/M7xUj1QpGgI, Accessed August 14, 2023.

[69]Candace Osmond, "Existential – Meaning & Definition," Grammarist, https://grammarist.com/usage/existential/accessed, August 17, 2023.

boundaries. This issue involves mass surveillance of public and potentially private places. When does facial, voice, and iris recognition move from a legitimate non-invasive, and voluntary business or law enforcement tool to an abusive government surveillance and control device? Will AI be used, even before the snatching up of the Church-Age saints at the Rapture, to track Christians, or other people groups thought to be a real or perceived threat by government agencies?

AI poses a serious challenge when considering the massive damage that could occur with personal, corporate, and government cyber-attacks. Virtually anyone with a computer uses anti-virus and malware detection software. Cyber-attacks are among the most feared and potentially damaging threats on a global scale. Every major area of life is in some way connected to a computer system. AI presently has a large presence in the world and could be used to negatively impact power grids, the flow of crude oil, private information, government classified information, and much more. The massive speed at which AI can process data and potentially hack through highly sensitive systems is a very real concern.

There are many other existential threats that AI poses. Consider the following list of areas where AI could have a serious negative impact: job displacement, lethal autonomous weapon proliferation, human enfeeblement and loss of meaning, mental health problems from harassment, social media addiction, social isolation, dehumanization of social interactions, threats to democracy, misinformation, and power concentration. Further, consider that AI could falsely accuse people of crimes, determine whether people find public housing, and prevent a qualified person from gaining employment based on biased resume screening. AI could cost someone their freedom by falsely identifying a suspect via a faulty facial recognition system.[70]

AI has great potential for good, but also for producing devastating results, including massive loss of life. What should the rule-of-law community do when considering this information? Individuals, corporations, and government agencies must stay informed about the development of AI and use their influence to warn about real and perceived dangers. The saying, all that has to

---

[70] "Six Dangers of AI! We Need to Pause it Now!" YouTube, https://youtu.be/M7xUj1QpGgI, Accessed August 14, 2023.

happen for evil to triumph is for good people to do nothing, rings true as AI continues to evolve.

AI Dependency a Sign of Devastation

Where does one draw the line when considering what tasks and problems a human being should attempt to solve, versus using an AI system? Developed, functioning AI systems can far outperform a human in many areas, from something as simple as playing chess to examining massive amounts of data to determine the cause of a genetic disorder. Consulting an AI system, in many cases, may be less expensive, faster, and smarter than consulting a person.

Companies that use old-fashioned pen and paper techniques to perform a myriad of tasks will find themselves quickly falling behind in a digital world. Those employing only basic computer applications that humans operate will also face a declining competitive edge when competing against businesses with advanced AI systems. Simply consider the massive rise in the number of consumers shopping from their home computer or smartphone instead of going to a brick-and-mortar store.

AI has also changed the way governments engage in warfare. The war between Russia and Ukraine brought to the public's attention the wartime use of AI.

> Ukraine's effective use of artificial intelligence (AI) to target Russian forces has pushed the technology onto the agenda of military and political leaders around the world, the CEO of U.S. software firm Palantir (PLTR.N) said... Speaking at the first international summit on responsible military use of AI, CEO Alex Karp said use of AI in war has moved from a "highly erudite ethics discussion" to a top concern since the start of the conflict in Ukraine. "This has now shifted to: your ability to identify the right technology and implement it will determine what happens on the battlefield," he said. "One of the major things we need to do in the West, is realize this lesson is completely understood by China and Russia."[71]

---

[71] Toby Sterling and Stephanie van den Berg, "Ukraine war shows urgency of military AI, Palantir CEO says," Reuters, February 15, 2023, https://www.reuters.com/technology/ukraine-war-shows-urgency-military-ai-palantir-ceo-says-2023-02-15/, accessed August 17, 2023.

The world is already dependent on the internet and digital applications. Virtually every area of life is in some way connected to digital technology. With the development of AI, large numbers of individuals, companies, and governments are taking advantage of the technology for a variety of purposes. The present culture desires instantaneous results for every query, from a simple word search to complex mathematical calculations. The case of someone failing to respond to a text message within a few seconds is intolerable. Making a post on social media without a massive number of *likes* is cause for depression.

Though placing a great deal of stock in AI may not result in human devastation, it is certainly a sign that humans are very accepting of advanced digital systems despite the risks. When the one-world system is in place, which is a biblical mandate during the Tribulation period, there is no doubt that when the image of the Antichrist speaks, people will listen.

Alignment of AI with Human Values

What are human values? Who has the authority to define what constitutes human values? How does a person, group, or government determine the definition and scope of human values? What is the definitive source for ethics and morality? There is no universally accepted answer to these questions.

The world is home to many religions and cultures, and there is a vast array of opinions on what constitutes human values. The issue of pro-life versus pro-choice accentuates the strong divergence of opinion on human values. One group is adamant that terminating a pregnancy (abortion) is murder, while the other side claims that abortion is simply removing a substance that has no human value. Can both positions be correct? The answer lies with what each person accepts in their life as the ultimate authority. Is the God of the Bible the ultimate authority? Is humanism, government, or one's conscience the ultimate authority, or does authority change based on situational ethics?

It is impossible to align AI with human values if humanity cannot agree on what they are. Those who doggedly hold to a biblical worldview, where every action must align with the principles found in Scripture, are never going to agree with the scope of human values defined by atheists, socialists, Marxists, communists, or those who will embrace the one-world system under Satan, Antichrist, and the false prophet.

Consider the following warning regarding the continued advancement of AI without stopping and determining how to safely proceed without harming humanity.

> We are developing AI in blind, which could lead to catastrophe for humanity. A misaligned AI system could pose existential risks to humanity, if it can surpass human capabilities before appropriate regulations are put in place... It is crucial to approach AI development with caution. There is a need for a comprehensive understanding of AI's capabilities and potential risks before advancing further. The unpredictability of future AI developments necessitates a careful examination of their impact on society, and the potential consequences for humanity. Only by prioritizing safety and ethical considerations can we navigate the complex landscape of AI and ensure a future that benefits rather than endangers humanity.[72]

The above warning is meaningless if those in leadership cannot reach a consensus regarding who or what is the ultimate authority. In a relativistic, pluralistic, inclusive, narcissistic, syncretistic, anything-goes culture, a consensus on what is good for humanity is impossible to reach. Therefore, the development of AI technology will continue in all probability with minimal regulation. Why? Because those in power around the world will seize every opportunity to stay in power by whatever means is necessary.

> He *(Antichrist)* was granted power to give breath to the image of the beast, that the image of the beast should both speak and cause as many as would not worship the image of the beast to be killed. He causes all, both small and great, rich and poor, free and slave, to receive a mark on their right hand or on their foreheads, and that no one may buy or sell except one who has the mark or the name of the beast, or the number of his name. (Rev. 13:15–17)

---

[72] "Six Dangers of AI! We Need to Pause it Now!" YouTube, https://youtu.be/M7xUj1QpGgI, Accessed August 14, 2023.

CHAPTER FOUR
TRANSHUMANISM
Introduction to Transhumanism

Virtually every young person daydreams about having superhuman powers. How can they watch the plethora of movies, TV shows, and internet videos that taunt viewers with the thrill of a superhuman body, and not desire those abilities for themselves? Well, the dawn of a new era is upon us. The advancement of technology, in a multiplicity of areas, has spawned the reality of mere human beings gaining capabilities once thought improbable.

Transhumanism is the ultimate vision of those seeking to live a more robust life, free from the diseases, limitations, and pains of the normal human body. In addition, people embrace the possibility of acquiring abilities beyond those of the normal human body. For example, within the animal kingdom there are many traits that far exceed those of humans, such as the speed of a cheetah, the visual acuity of an eagle, the strength of a lion or bear, the muscle structure of a gorilla, the swimming ability of a seal, and the agility and balance of a mountain goat; the list goes on and on. Add to this the one top-tier objective for the transhumanist: to gain immortality through scientific means.

The strongest instinct of virtually every person is survival. People want to live for many reasons, but one of the greatest motivators for survival is the fear of death. People have many questions surrounding death, and what that process entails. Some individuals claim they experienced death and come back to life. A few of them have written books and conducted interviews, relating their stories. What these select individuals state as fact is certainly open to interpretation. Even the Bible does not explain the intricacies of the dying process. Death is an assumed process in Scripture, which every person, with few exceptions, will experience. The biblical exceptions to the mandate that all will die (Rom. 5:12; Heb. 9:27), include Enoch and Elijah, whom God took to heaven (Gen. 5:24; 2 Kings 2:1-12), and a yet future group of Christians, as of the writing of this book, known as the Church-Age saints, or the body of Christ, who will not die. Jesus will snatch away or catch up to heaven one generation of Christians who will escape death (1 Thess. 4:13-18; 1 Cor. 15:50-54). The last chapter of this book describes this issue in depth in the context of God's prophetic chronological timeline.

Humanity is fascinated with the possibility of improving the performance and longevity of life through science and technology, leading to the concept of transhumanism. Britannica defines transhumanism as follows.

> Transhumanism: a philosophical and scientific movement that advocates the use of current and emerging technologies—such as genetic engineering, cryonics, artificial intelligence (AI), and nanotechnology—to augment human capabilities and improve the human condition. Transhumanists envision a future in which the responsible application of such technologies enables humans to slow, reverse, or eliminate the aging process, to achieve corresponding increases in human life spans, and to enhance human cognitive and sensory capacities. The movement proposes that humans with augmented capabilities will evolve into an enhanced species that transcends humanity—the "posthuman."[73]

The current generation has made great strides towards transhumanism due to recent developments and significant research funding. However, the move towards transhumanism is not new; it has been a topic of discussion for decades. Once again, Britannica offers excellent information on this subject.

> The term *transhumanism* was popularized by the English biologist and philosopher Julian Huxley in his 1957 essay of the same name. Huxley held that it was now possible for social institutions to supplant human evolution in refining and improving the human species. Although Huxley was principally concerned with advancing the human condition through social and cultural change, the general notion of humanity transcending itself came to be adopted by the emerging transhumanist movement, which coalesced around significant scientific advances, such as the development of computer technology, the advent of space travel, and the

---

[73] René Ostberg,. "transhumanism". Encyclopedia Britannica, 3 Nov. 2022, https://www.britannica.com/topic/transhumanism. Accessed 20 August 2023.

successful use of cryopreservation (e.g., of human eggs and embryos).[74]

The tremendous rise in the number of ultra-rich and powerful people in the world, who have a keen interest in a high quality of life and longevity, has sparked an increase in the number of resources and research dedicated to AI and transhumanism. These vast resources now allow for that which was previously impossible to achieve. In addition, there is a significant cultural move away from a biblical worldview. In the past people accepted the Scriptural position that life must end at some point. Those who hold even loosely to a biblical worldview, anticipated that they would *rest in peace*, or go to a place called *heaven* to live with God. There is now a significant move away from the Scriptures, and an increasing number of people who refuse to accept the existence of God, or if they do, that He will guarantee them a wonderful life after death. Many people do not accept things by biblical faith; they desire concrete, tangible evidence of what their future entails. Therefore, transhumanism is continually gaining popularity among those who have the means to develop it.

Transhumanism found further support from Silicon Valley entrepreneurs, including Google co-founder Larry Page, Amazon's Jeff Bezos, and Tesla's Elon Musk. In 2013 Page launched Calico Life Sciences LLC (Calico Labs), a research and development company dedicated to extending the human life span through advanced technologies. In early 2022 Bezos and other backers invested $3 billion in Altos Labs, a biotechnology company seeking to reverse aging and disease. Musk founded SpaceX in 2002 in hopes of establishing human colonies on the Moon and Mars and launched Neuralink in 2016 to develop implantable brain chips. In July 2022 the brain chip company Synchron announced that it had successfully implanted a chip in the brain of an ALS (amyotrophic lateral sclerosis) patient in the United States. The chip was designed to enable severely

---

[74]René Ostberg,. "transhumanism". Encyclopedia Britannica, 3 Nov. 2022, https://www.britannica.com/topic/transhumanism. Accessed 20 August 2023.

paralyzed patients to operate digital forms of communication with their thoughts.[75]

Transhumanism provides the possible venue for how the satanic trinity will accomplish the formation of the dictatorial one-world government, economy, and religion, and how the image of the beast will enforce the mandates. Specifically, transhumanism may be how the image of the Antichrist, also called the *image of the beast*, will possess the ability to perform tasks that appear to be outside of the scope of current technology.

> "He *(false prophet)* was granted power to give breath to the image of the beast, that the image of the beast should both speak and cause as many as would not worship the image of the beast to be killed. He causes all, both small and great, rich and poor, free and slave, to receive a mark on their right hand or on their foreheads, and that no one may buy or sell except one who has the mark or the name of the beast, or the number of his name. (Rev. 13:15–17)

Though the technology to implant a digital chip into human beings to control who can or cannot sell or purchase products already exists, the technology to determine, on a global basis, who is worshipping an image, and then execute those who refuse to do so, does not exist.

The select groups researching transhumanism provide technical and philosophical thoughts regarding its development. The secular and religious sectors of the world should realize that transhumanism is starting to play a significant role in society, with many positive developments as well as some that could result in tragic outcomes. Consider the following information from author Jacob Shatzer.

> So, where does the interaction between the two--between technology itself and the human being--lead us? How is it shaping us? I argue that much of modern technology tends towards a transhuman future, a future created by the next stage of evolution (the post human), moving beyond what it currently means to be human. This argument might initially startle you: most people would not say they want to become posthuman, or to have their brains uploaded to a computer,

---

[75] René Ostberg, "transhumanism". Encyclopedia Britannica, 3 Nov. 2022, https://www.britannica.com/topic/transhumanism. Accessed 20 August 2023.

or some other sci-fi scenario. Yet technology disciples us. And if we look closely, we can see that uncritical use of technology can shape us to be more attracted to transhumanism than we might think we are--or want to be.[76]

Shatzer's statement that "technology disciples us," opens a myriad of philosophical considerations. Webster defines *disciple* as, "one who accepts and assists in spreading the doctrines of another."[77] In addition, consider the loaded meaning behind the synonyms of disciple, and their suggested adherents.

> FOLLOWER, ADHERENT, DISCIPLE, PARTISAN mean one who gives full loyalty and support to another.
> FOLLOWER may apply to people who attach themselves either to the person or beliefs of another.
> Example: an evangelist and his *followers*
> ADHERENT suggests a close and persistent attachment.
> Example: *adherents* to Marxism
> DISCIPLE implies a devoted allegiance to the teachings of one chosen as a master.
> Example: *disciples* of Gandhi[78]

Should we elevate technology to the position of a *master receiving devoted allegiance*? Should we give our allegiance to technology, specifically something developed by the transhumanists, as Marxism requires? These questions will require real answers from real people when the prophetic scenario in Revelation 13 becomes a life-threatening reality. Will people living during the last half of the seven-year Tribulation decide to receive the Lord Jesus Christ as their personal Savior, and face almost certain martyrdom, or will they bow the knee to the satanic image of the beast, reject Jesus, and face the eternal separation from their Creator in the lake of fire (Rev. 21:8)? Transhumanism may be the means by which Satan runs portions of his global empire, but God Himself will never be overruled by the deceptive, anti-God tactics of the satanic trinity.

---

[76] Jacob Shatzer, *Transhumanism and the Image of God* (Downers Grove, IL.: IVP Academics, 2019), 10.

[77] "Disciple," Merriam-Webster.com Dictionary, s.v., https://www.merriam-webster.com/dictionary/disciples, accessed August 21, 2023.

[78] Ibid.

Shatzer provides additional information on transhumanism as it relates to posthumanism.

> Transhumanism and posthumanism are two related philosophies tied closely to the promises of technology. Posthumanism argues that there is a new stage in human evolution. In this stage, humans will become posthuman because of our interaction with and connection to technology. Transhumanism, on the other hand, promotes values that contribute to this change. Transhumanism aims at posthumanism, and both are based to a large degree on the potential offered by technology. In a way, transhumanism provides the thinking and method for moving toward posthumanism. Transhumanism leads to posthumanism. They share a common value system…. Understanding the values of posthumanism is not an end in itself.[79]

The philosophical issue presented by Shatzer crosses the line of biblical Christianity to suggest that transhumanism will eventually lead to posthumanism, or in essence, a new species that will co-exist with, or potentially eradicate humanity. This statement alone should shock the conscience of every rational person. Yes, science and technology produce things once thought impossible, but they cannot go beyond the bounds of the sovereign God. Consider the following information on posthumanism.

> Post-humanism, which is a set of ideas that have been emerging since around the 1990s, challenges the notion that humans are and always will be the only agents of the moral world. In fact, post-humanists argue that in our technologically mediated future, understanding the world as a moral hierarchy and placing humans at the top of it will no longer make sense. The best-known post-humanists, who are also sometimes referred to as transhumanists, claim that in the coming century, human beings will be radically altered by implants, bio-hacking, cognitive enhancement, and other bio-medical technology. These enhancements will lead us to "evolve" into a species that is completely unrecognizable to what we are now. This vision of the future is championed

---

[79] Jacob Shatzer, *Transhumanism and the Image of God* (Downers Grove, IL.: IVP Academics, 2019), 12.

most vocally by Ray Kurzweil, a chief engineer of Google, who believes that the exponential rate of technological development will bring an end to human history as we have known it, triggering completely new ways of being that mere mortals like us cannot yet comprehend.[80]

Though technology and science will absolutely bring that which was once thought impossible into existence, humanity will never face extinction, based on the truth of the infallible Scriptures. God's Word, the Bible, does not allow for the extinction of humanity. However, there is a significant amount of latitude given to Satan and his demonic army of fallen angels, to cause massive deception and carnage on the earth. Very few people, including some Christians, comprehend the meaning of 2 Corinthians 4:4 which states, "But even if our gospel is veiled, it is veiled to those who are perishing, whose minds the god of this age has blinded, who do not believe, lest the light of the gospel of the glory of Christ, who is the image of God, should shine on them." The translators of the English Bible rightly did not capitalize the word *god* in that verse. There is only one true God, and there is no other (Gen. 1:1; Deut. 4:35, 6:4; Isa. 44:6, 45:5). Therefore, as the discussion continues regarding transhumanism, posthumanism, and all the potential developments, one should never forget that everything God allows aligns with His sovereign will, which is to care for His children, and to judge those who refuse to place their faith in the sacrificial work accomplished by the Lord Jesus Christ, through His death, burial, and resurrection (1 Cor. 15:1-4).

Transhumanism – Advanced Prosthetic Devices

The development of prosthetic devices is one major example of new technology that could one day lead to transhumanism. Newly developed prosthetics allow people who have lost limbs to not only have what appears to be a semi-functioning limb but also one that allows the user to experience feelings or sensations. In 2021 the following startling information appeared on the internet regarding the technological advancements in prosthetic devices.

---

[80] "Ethics Explainer: Post-Humanism," The Ethics Center, February 22, 2018, https://ethics.org.au/ethics-explainer-post-humanism/,accessed August 21, 2023.

Additive manufacturing, or 3D printing, has reduced prosthetics' prototyping, customization, and production costs while advances in neuroscience have revealed tantalizing clues about how the brain processes sensations of touch, pressure, temperature, and pain. From prosthetic hands that can replicate 100 different sensations to exoskeletons that will respond to changing terrain in real time—a potential boon for patients with spinal cord injuries—scientists have been exploring ways to make prosthetics feel and behave like the real thing. And as these assistive technologies improve, so do people's lives.[81]

This new technology is wonderful news for anyone who has suffered the loss of a limb or was born without one or more limbs. By no means should we consider these advancements in technology and science anything but a blessing for those who enjoy the benefits. God allows many wonderful inventions and developments to enhance the lives of people. Consider the following astounding development in prosthetic devices for arms and hands.

New Thought-Controlled Prosthetics Restore the Sensation of Touch

Star Wars fans will remember Luke Skywalker's bionic hand responding to the probes of a medical robot in *The Empire Strikes Back*, a scene that left many viewers wondering when science fiction might become reality. Now, more than 40 years after that scene was shot, researchers at the University of Utah—using a prosthetic arm named, you guessed it, the LUKE—have figured out a way to restore more than 100 sensations to amputees. By implanting a device into a person's residual nerves, as well as electrodes placed in muscles, the researchers have created an information loop that is then transferred into signals that the brain recognizes as sensations of touch.[82]

---

[81]Mark Smith, "Breakthroughs in Prosthetic Technology Promise Better Living Through Design," October 6, 2021, https://redshift.autodesk.com/articles/prosthetic-technology, accessed August 20, 2023.

[82] Ibid.

Current hand prostheses can only target a couple hundred of the more than 10,000 nerves in the hand, limiting what they can do.[83] However, to a person who formerly had no ability to sense or feel something with their arm or hand, this technology is amazing. The issue is not to in any way impede progress for the betterment of humanity but to guard against the potential misuse of technology to advance outcomes that will negatively impact society. Such is the warning given throughout this research, that in the prophetic future, that which God originally designed for good, and resulted in astoundingly wonderful benefits, will eventually be flipped into something that the satanic-led world will use for enormous deception and harm to humanity (Matt. 24:4, 5, 11, 24; Rev. 13).

Scientists, using advanced technology, have developed prosthetic legs that now provide much more realistic movement and sensations. Once again, the Christian and secular communities should be excited about these wonderful advancements for those who use them. The following is a thrilling report regarding these medical advancements.

> Researchers implanted a device into the legs of three individuals with lower limb amputations. The device included a sensor that records pressure information from the robotic foot during walking and electrodes implanted into the peripheral nerves of the leg. It effectively "senses" the walking sensations and transmits that information into the amputee's nervous system to try to mimic the sensations associated with walking.
>
> To see which type of stimulation felt more natural, the researchers applied either biomimetic stimulation from the model or a steady stream of electric pulses. Participants rated the biomimetic stimulation as feeling more natural. When they got the steady stream of pulses, "they would say things like 'I felt like my leg was plugged into the electricity', which we, of course, want to avoid," says Stanisa Raspopovic, a neuroengineer at ETH Zürich and co-author of the study.
>
> The amputees were able to walk up and down stairs faster with the biomimetic stimulation than with the constant

---

[83] Claudia López Lloreda "Nerve-Mimicking Device Gives 'Feeling' To Prosthetics," Science, July 28, 2023, https://www.science.org/content/article/nerve-mimicking-device-gives-feeling-prosthetics, accessed August 20, 2023.

stimulation, being able to complete about half a lap more of the circuit in each session. When asked after the task, participants said they felt more confident when walking with the natural stimulation. Finally, when the researchers asked the volunteers to spell a five-letter word backward while they were walking, their spelling was about 20% more accurate during biomimetic stimulation.
A more detailed understanding of how the nervous system detects and communicates the different aspects of touch could help further refine such devices. Sensations such as pressure, pain, and temperature could help the researchers create a sensory experience that more closely resembles reality and eventually feels identical to the lost limb, for example, Clark says. "That's the idea—you want people to feel whole again."[84]

The development of advanced prosthetic devices opens a wide door of opportunity for taking the body to a new technological level. The extent to which such devices could be used, not only for those who have lost appendages but potentially for improving the capabilities of those who have their appendages intact, is yet to be realized.

Transhumanism – Supernatural Sensory Perception

"Consider what it would be like to be able to hear distant sounds, see thousands of things at once, and read everything ever published. You can slow it down to sampling this material in a leisurely manner. The scenario is similar to how the synthetic intellects work."[85] Scientists, technology experts, government agencies, and well-resourced companies and individuals currently have the ability, through the use of telescopes, microscopes, sound enhancement, and other advanced tools to enhance a person's ability to see and hear things beyond the normal scope of the human

---

[84] Claudia López Lloreda "Nerve-Mimicking Device Gives 'Feeling' To Prosthetics," Science, July 28, 2023, https://www.science.org/content/article/nerve-mimicking-device-gives-feeling-prosthetics, accessed August 20, 2023.

[85] Jacob Shatzer, *Transhumanism and the Image of God* (Downers Grove, IL.: IVP Academics, 2019), 91-92.

ears, eyes, and other senses. The vision of the transhumanist is to take the large devices and computers needed to operate standalone machines and condense them to the point where they could be implanted or attached to a person, giving the person supernatural capabilities.

Consider something as simple as a hearing aid. Users simply place the tiny devices into their ears and adjust the control to their desired hearing level. Now go beyond the simple detachable hearing aid and consider the technology behind cochlear implants. The device requires a surgical process that is specific to those who have profound hearing loss, resulting from damaged follicles in the inner ear. The cochlear implant sends electronic impulses to the brain, where the brain interprets the impulses as sounds. There are two main components to the implant. First, there is an external microphone, sound processor, and transmitter. Second, there is a surgically implanted receiver and electrode that contains electronic circuits which receive signals from the externally worn equipment, which finally sends electronic current to the inner ear. "The cochlear implant receives sound from the outside environment, processes it, and sends small electric currents near the auditory nerve. These electric currents activate the nerve, which then sends a signal to the brain. The brain learns to recognize this signal and the person experiences this as hearing. The cochlear implant somewhat simulates natural hearing, where sound creates an electric current that stimulates the auditory nerve."[86]

The developments in hearing technology are impressive. Now imagine if all the human senses had electronic enhancements that gave them supernatural abilities. Consider the possibility of infrared vision, x-ray vision, the ability to see things clearly miles away, or closeup vision that mimics a high-powered microscope. Science and technology experts are continually at work on these concepts. Though the advancements have yet to reach the superhuman level, there are certainly many devices already in production that assist those with impaired senses to have improved ability, and therefore, an improved quality of life.

---

[86] "What is a Cochlear Implant?" FDA, February 4, 2018, https://www.fda.gov/medical-devices/cochlear-implants/what-cochlear-implant#:~:text=A%20cochlear%20implant%20receives%20sound,experiences%20this%20as%20%22hearing%22, accessed August 21, 2023.

When considering the current advancements in sensory technology, curious minds should consider the very real probability that some form of transhumanism could perform the functions assigned to *the image of the beast* in Revelation 13:15-17. There are certainly many alarmists, sensationalists, charlatans, conspiracy theorists, and others who exploit this type of information for personal reasons. There are also those, such as myself, who are interested in the advancement of truth, and the provision of a calculated warning. Sleepy attitudes, status quo thinking, complacency, and a lack of a sense of urgency lead to disastrous results, which is a prophetic certainty when the global deception becomes a reality under the satanically charged rein of the Antichrist and the false prophet.

No single human being possesses the abilities that the Scriptures state the image of the beast will possess. However, based on God's perfect record up to the current day of fulfilling 500 biblical prophecies exactly as written, we can be certain He will also bring even the hard-to-comprehend scenario in Revelation 13 to fulfillment.

Transhumanism and Artificial General Intelligence

There are numerous ways that transhumanism could impact globalism in the future. An excellent video, "Transhumanism, 20 Ways It will Change the World" by Future Business Tech, provides a list of things that are interesting, yet have potentially serious implications. The first projection on their list is that artificial intelligence could merge with transhumanism. The author speculates that if AI advances to the level of intelligent AI, which exceeds the abilities of artificial general intelligence (AGI), the currently unimaginable levels of human intelligence will become a reality.

This will allow us to connect our minds to advanced artificial intelligence, and the entire internet. We will be able to solve the most complex problems in existence in real-time. We could view the world mathematically, and understand it in ways that non-enhanced humans cannot begin to understand. And we could run simulations accounting for trillions of factors at a time, and generate predictions with pinpoint accuracy. **Our levels of intelligence would increase by so much it would like we transcended to an entirely**

different species, and this will only get better as brain-computer interfaces become more advanced, internet speeds improve, and AIs become exponentially more intelligent. **When humans start using synthetic brains,** we could potentially make ourselves trillions of times more intelligent than the typical human being. People in career paths such as research, physics, and engineering could have exclusive access to the most advanced versions of these AI emerging technologies.[87]

Consider the implications regarding the alleged formation of a *new species*. Regardless of whether there is any possibility of that concept materializing, the fact is that there are well-resourced people and organizations that are attempting to make the new species a reality. The more one examines current events in the light of Bible prophecy, the more sense passages such as Revelation 13 make.

Jacob Shatzer suggests the possibility of an AGI system that involves a combination of the human brain and AGI, and then he takes the concept a step further by stating that developers could link multiple brains to make what he calls a global brain.

"Researchers envision utilizing AGI in a few different ways. First, individual human minds could interface with an AGI to create a human hybrid brain. Second, AGI could network together various human minds and artificial intelligence to create what some call a global brain or multiple competing brains."[88]

"AGI" also plays a key role in developing what some researchers call the emerging global brain as mentioned above. This idea stems from the observation that the various human minds on the earth are gradually becoming more connected into a greater mind. This observation depends on a definition of mind that emphasizes the connection between various neurons in the human brain and expanding that to include connections between brains. In other words, a human

---

[87]"Transhumanism: 20 Ways It Will Change the World," Future Business Tech, YouTube, https://www.youtube.com/watch?v=qcsihbGnXgE, accessed June 7, 2023.

[88] Jacob Shatzer, *Transhumanism and the Image of God* (Downers Grove, IL.: IVP Academics, 2019), 93-94.

brain is a connection of neurons. Thus, a global brain would be a connection of brains or an extended connection of neurons between biological and technological systems and interfaces. Such an AGI could be quite powerful indeed, and give rise to even more powerful intelligences. Not all thinkers agree that this will be seamless and peaceful. In fact, one of the important pieces of the development will be whether one powerful AI is developed or various competing AIs at similar paces, leading to competition or outright conflict. In transhumanist thinking, this increase will lead to what some call the intelligence explosion."[89]

The pursuit to combine a powerful AGI with a human brain accentuates man's desire to advance to an extremely high intellectual level. On its face, becoming the best one can be appears to be a positive action. However, what is the motivation and actual goal of those seeking superhuman abilities?

Satan's desire has been the destruction of his Creator since the beginning of biblical times. He actively targeted Eve, the first woman created by God, and made his plea for her to reject God's command not to eat of the tree of the knowledge of good and evil. Satan made the following deceptive and tempting appeal to Eve. "Then the serpent said to the woman, "You will not surely die. For God knows that in the day you eat of it your eyes will be opened, and you will be like God, knowing good and evil" (Gen. 3:4–5). Satan's two statements, which were both lies, tricked Eve into making the fatal decision that would lead to her husband, Adam, also disobeying God. Their direct disobedience to God resulted in physical and spiritual death for all of Adam's descendants, which includes every single person ever born, except Jesus, who was virgin born (Isa. 7:14). What was the great promise of Satan to Eve? "You will be like God." What a promise! What a temptation! "You will be like God."

What is the ultimate desire of those who reject the Scriptures and have no understanding of what will happen to them at death? They want to live forever and become a god. AGI and transhumanism provide the potential road map to obtain what humanity has sought, apart from God, since the creation of Adam and Eve, which is for their

---

[89] Jacob Shatzer, *Transhumanism and the Image of God* (Downers Grove, IL.: IVP Academics, 2019), 96-97.

human body to have eternal life, and to obtain God-like abilities. There are certainly exceptions to this general statement, including those who embrace a religion, or those who have a personal relationship with Jesus Christ and have accepted the gift of eternal life through faith in His death, burial, and resurrection as the complete payment for their sins (1 Cor. 15:3-4; Eph. 2:8-9; Titus 3:5-6). However, Satan's deceptive attacks appear to be increasing at an exponential rate, as he attempts to deceive as many as possible into accepting a system that will result in the ruination of society as a whole, in the establishment of the one-world government, economy, and religion (Rev. 13).

Transhumanism and Ethics

Ethics is often compared with morals, and the definition of each word is contingent on the personal beliefs and worldview of the one using it. The following comparison from MasterClass provides an interesting starting point. "Ethical standards are distinct from moral principles, though the two may overlap. The terms "moral" and "ethical" also have different etymological origins. While "mos," meaning "customs," is the Latin root word of moral, the etymology of ethical traces back to the ancient Greek word "ethos," meaning "character.'"[90]

Before discussing the ethics of transhumanism, it will be helpful to better understand the difference between ethics and morality. MasterClass defines the difference as follows. "Moral rules are personal and vary from individual to individual. While your actions and moral beliefs may remain consistent, your moral behaviors can differ greatly from the behavior of others. Ethical principles remain consistent across industries and institutions, as they offer strict behavioral guidelines. For example, the code of professional ethics for two doctors living in different cities is the same despite their geographic differences."[91] The MasterClass definition of morals is true from a secular perspective, which is certainly the dominant worldview. However, from a biblical perspective, the definition falls short of God's standard for morality,

---

[90] "Moral vs. Ethical: 3 Differences Between Ethics and Morals, MasterClass," October 23, 2022, https://www.masterclass.com/articles/moral-vs-ethical, accessed August 22, 2023.

[91] Ibid.

which God specifically commands throughout the Scriptures. This difference accentuates the acute problem between humanists and Biblicists. Is attempting to become a god, or replace humanity with an AGI system, moral and ethical? The answer depends on one's worldview.

A second area of contrast between morals and ethics is in the area of decision making. Once again, we turn to MasterClass for their take on this issue. "Both your moral values and code of ethics influence your decision making daily. Moral decisions stem from personal values, so choosing to help a friend results from the importance you place on friendship. However, when you encounter an ethical issue, your code of ethical behavior influences your response. For example, a defense lawyer chooses to defend their client even if it contradicts their moral beliefs due to their ethical code as a lawyer."[92] Therefore, according to the MasterClass definition, one's moral beliefs are rock solid, whereas one's ethics are adapted to the situation; this is commonly known as situational ethics. With all due respect to defense attorneys, they do make a moral decision to defend those they know are guilty; yet by law, they must defend the guilty person to the best of their ability.

The question is, why would one choose a profession where you know you are performing a service that could lead to a disastrous and dangerous outcome? Why would you defend a serial rapist, an admitted pedophile, or a person who told you (their lawyer) they were guilty of the homicide for which they are on trial? Why not do the right moral thing and plead guilty? Why would a person, group, corporation, or government agency create a domineering AGI system that demands worship, and controls every aspect of a person's life, including their ability to buy or sell, and who they will worship, with the threat of death for those who refuse? Morals and ethics as defined by the humanist, secularist, socialist, Marxist, communist, atheists, and all others who reject the totality of the Scriptures, will all dramatically differ from those who embrace a biblical worldview.

MasterClass provides a third area to consider when discussing the difference between morals and ethics, which they refer to as "governing factors." "Different contexts influence morality and ethics. Ethical rules stem from a social context since they relate to societal regulations—an entire community or

---

[92]Ibid.

organization establishes a set of ethical beliefs to decide what is right and wrong collectively. On the other hand, moral codes exist on a personal level, as individuals internalize a set of values to create their own concept of what is morally correct."[93] This is the exact issue with which the developers of AI must grapple. When moral code is determined individually, or by a specific group of like-minded developers, chaos can ensue. When the culture deems murder morally acceptable, violence permeates society. When society believes that stealing from others is acceptable, based on a person's needs, burglary and robbery become acceptable. When a world dictator, emboldened by Satan, determines that every person will worship his image or face execution, then that is exactly what will occur, as that practice is the dictator's personally accepted moral and subsequently ethical position.

The challenge remains that if society cannot agree on a specific definition of ethics, then attempting to determine what is right and wrong is impossible. Britannica provides an excellent summary of the issue.

> As transhumanist ideas developed from theory to actuality in the late 20th and early 21st centuries, ethical concerns increasingly took a central role in transhumanist philosophy. Scientific breakthroughs—including stem cell therapies, in vitro fertilization, brain chips, animal cloning, exoskeletons (e.g., robotic arms), artificial intelligence, and genomics—have redirected the dialogue between transhumanism's proponents and its critics from the future to the present.
>
> Advocates of transhumanism argue that emerging technologies can be used to eliminate disease and otherwise improve human life as well as to provide solutions for urgent global problems. For example, brain chips and "mind uploading"—initially the fanciful dreams of those seeking a form of infinite intelligence or immortality through the computerized extension of consciousness—might be used to cure or overcome neurological disorders such as dementia, Alzheimer's disease, and paralysis. Likewise, the likely catastrophic effects of climate change have spurred some transhumanists to promote space colonization. Critics

---

[93]Ibid.

have countered that realizing the transhumanist goal of slowing or reversing aging and extending human life spans will only worsen overpopulation—to which a transhumanist may reassert the necessity of establishing human colonies on Mars.

Based on the above-stated conflicts between proponents and critics of various real and potential advancements in transhumanism, the obvious challenges remain, specifically defining what is right and wrong, what is ethical, and what is moral. The conflict between good and evil in the form of Satan versus God has existed since the dawn of creation and is not going away until God literally puts an end to this sin-cursed world, and humanity enters eternity. (The final chapter of this book addresses God's prophetic timeline.)

The debate regarding the ethical concerns of transhumanism is further addressed in the Britannica article as follows.

Concerns that transhumanist technology will create greater social inequities are among the most-voiced criticisms of the movement. In an article published in the journal *Foreign Policy* in 2004, the American political theorist Francis Fukuyama called transhumanism "the world's most dangerous idea," warning that biotechnology's offerings might come at a "frightful moral cost" to human rights. Fukuyama pointed out that wide economic disparities between countries may further encourage "enhanced" individuals to claim superior rights to "those left behind."

Transhumanism continues to be compared to the eugenics movement, reflecting fears that technology will be exploited by those wishing to become or breed "superhumans." For example, the synthetic production of hormones such as erythropoietin, which is naturally produced in the kidneys and increases the production of red blood cells, and adaptive technology such as bionic implants and carbon-fiber prosthetics are sought out not only by people with blood disorders or disabilities but also by nondisabled athletes looking to boost their performance. Conversely, transhumanists may argue that genetic engineering has long been practiced in agriculture and animal breeding, resulting in features of modern life that are largely accepted, from sweet corn to domestic dogs and cats.

Although transhumanism has been characterized as a materialist and atheist or agnostic
philosophy, some transhumanists have espoused theories that resemble or even adapt New Age, Buddhist, or Christian beliefs. In *The Physics of Immortality* (1994), for example, the American physicist Frank Tipler borrowed from the French Jesuit theologian and paleontologist Pierre Teilhard de Chardin's Omega point theory—which proposes that evolution is converging toward a final unity—to present a concept of God as a cosmic computerized intelligence that is equivalent to the Omega. When the Omega point is reached, everyone will experience a computational resurrection into immortality.

In *The Age of Spiritual Machines* (1999), the American futurist and computer scientist Ray Kurzweil predicted that machines will not only overtake human intelligence but will appear to develop free will and have emotional and spiritual experiences. In *The Singularity Is Near* (2005), Kurzweil expanded on this theory to predict an impending singularity, in which human intelligence will merge with artificial intelligence and all disease, aging, social ills, and death will be reversed, resolved, or eliminated. Kurzweil predicted that the singularity will be reached by 2045.[94]

A major goal of transhumanism is reversing the aging process. Research scientists invest countless hours and massive resources attempting to prolong life. However, though scientists have made significant advancements, and many lives that otherwise would have been cut short have reached normal life spans, no one has determined how to prolong life into the hundreds of years. The Guinness Book of Records states the oldest known person (who has died) was Jeanne Louise Calment of France, who lived 122 years and 164 days.[95] Despite modern medical advancements, no one in recent history has surpassed the longevity of Mrs. Calment, set on August 4, 1997.

---

[94] René Ostberg, "transhumanism". Encyclopedia Britannica, 3 Nov. 2022, https://www.britannica.com/topic/transhumanism. Accessed 20 August 2023.

[95] Dominic Punt, "The World's Oldest People and Their Secrets to a Long Life," accessed August 8, 22, 2023.

The following represents the transhumanist goal of attempting to reverse the aging process and prolong life.

Because of the technological advancements in fields such as genetic engineering, and nanotechnology, we could potentially live for hundreds of years. This would enable us to live long enough to use some of the most advanced futuristic technologies that many people today claim will never exist. And we would see societies change in ways that are perhaps incredibly shocking to us. Accomplishing this would involve identifying peak genes and molecular pathways that could be targeted to slow or reverse the effects of time on our bodies. Additionally, nanobots could continually repair cellular damage at the molecular level, effectively combating the root causes of aging from within. Then as we live longer, we would swap out our body organs for new versions that are considerably more advanced and durable.[96]

Though science and technology played a part in keeping many people alive who would otherwise have died without medical attention, the fact remains that God has mandated that people will not live past the body's current physical limitations. The Bible records that the person who lived the longest far exceeded the life span of Mrs. Calment at a mere 122 years. Genesis 5:27 states that Methuselah lived 969 years. Genesis further documents that Adam, the first male created by God lived 930 years. Adam's son Seth lived 912 years. Noah, the builder of the ark, lived 950 years. Why do human beings now die at a significantly younger age? The answer is that God determined He would reduce the number of years all humans would live, based on their sinfulness. "The days of our lives are seventy years; And if by reason of strength they are eighty years, yet their boast is only labor and sorrow; for it is soon cut off, and we fly away" (Psalm 90:10).

The biblical reality is that the wishful thinking of the AI and transhumanist developers to gain immortality in their current or significantly modified bodies and override the infallible Scriptures is literal foolishness. When the satanic trinity comes to power at the midpoint of the prophetic seven-year Tribulation, dying becomes the

---

[96] "Transhumanism: 20 Ways It Will Change the World," Future Business Tech, YouTube, https://www.youtube.com/watch?v=qcsihbGnXgE, accessed June 7, 2023.

norm, not the exception. As stated earlier, the biblical prophecy is that well over 50% of the world's population perishes during the seven-year Tribulation, due to violence, lawlessness, wars, disease, pestilence, and other judgments of God, which provides no allowance for the transhumanist dream to materialize (Matt. 24; Rev. 6-16).

The only point of agreement between the biblical account of the future and that of the AI and transhumanist developers is that there absolutely will be an image of the Antichrist developed that will have what appears to be supernatural abilities. In addition, AI technology already exists for chip implants for hands, which feasibly a government agency or private corporation could also develop to be implanted in people's foreheads.

> He *(false prophet)* was granted power to give breath to the image of the beast, that the image of the beast should both speak and cause as many as would not worship the image of the beast to be killed. He causes all, both small and great, rich and poor, free and slave,to receive a mark on their right hand or on their foreheads, and that no one may buy or sell except one who has the mark or the name of the beast, or the number of his name.
> (Rev. 13:15–17)

The AI and transhumanist concept of people gaining extended life, due to scientific and technological developments, finds no allowance in the Scriptures. In fact, the greatest issue in the future is the ability to survive in a totally chaotic world. There will be future peace and longevity of life due to the prophetic certainty of Jesus Christ coming physically back to this earth, at the completion of the horrible seven-year Tribulation. After Jesus purges the earth of all that is evil, including the removal of Satan, Antichrist, and the false prophet (Rev. 19:20-20:3), Jesus will inaugurate His one-thousand-year theocratic kingdom. Upon the return of the Lord Jesus Christ, He will take His throne in Jerusalem as the King of kings and Lord of lords (Isa. 9:6-7; Zech. 14:1-5; Rev. 19:11-20:7). The lifespan of people will dramatically increase during Christ's millennial kingdom, not because of AI or transhumanism, but because Jesus will reverse many aspects of the judgments God placed on the world immediately after Adam and Eve disobeyed God (Gen. 3:16-19; Isa. 11:6; 65:20-25).

CHAPTER FIVE
TRANSHUMANISM AND DEVELOPER'S VISION

The major goals of transhumanism are all oriented toward developing technologies that give humans the ability to do more than ever thought possible. Many of the desired goals have tremendous value for people with disabilities or health issues, as well as for those seeking a competitive edge. Human competition takes place in virtually every area of life. People train rigorously to master various sports, music, games, and other endeavors. In addition, those who desire a professional career that pays well find out quickly that acceptance in the best colleges and universities is highly competitive and expensive. If someone is fortunate enough to gain entrance into a respected institution of higher learning, the competition between students becomes another hurdle to overcome. The student who graduates then enters the job market, where candidates compete for the most prized positions. Can the competitive world become a place where more people have a greater opportunity to succeed in the areas in which they wish to participate?

Consider the benefits to national security if soldiers possessed capabilities that far exceeded those of their enemies. The scenarios in which properly developed and monitored transhumanism could benefit society are endless. However, as previously stated, technologies that have the potential to benefit society could also be used to harm it.

This section examines the potential benefits as well as the potential harmful or unintended consequences of transhumanism. Biblical prophecy reveals horrific adverse outcomes that are yet to be fulfilled. Transhumanism may in fact be one of the tools that the satanic one-world system incorporates to accomplish its reign of terror described in Revelation 13.

Transhumanism and Superhuman Capabilities

Transhumanism developers look to incorporate genetic engineering that results in humans having super strength, intelligence, and attractiveness. Imagine possessing the ability to lift extremely heavy objects that normally would require the use of a mechanical device. Many athletes take performance-enhancing drugs to increase their muscle mass and strength. Researchers are currently exploring how to give athletes and others the strength they desire by altering their genetic structure.

Consider the tremendous edge military personnel would have if their genetics far exceeded their enemy's. Imagine having the ability to run extremely long distances at vehicular speeds, dramatically reducing the need for rigorous training. A genetically altered human being could potentially possess an IQ that exceeds the IQ of the most brilliant person who has ever lived. Transhumanism desires to develop such superhuman capabilities in people.

How could one think poorly of the transhumanist goal of making humans immune to thousands of diseases? Or question the desire to enhance human vision and hearing, and senses of smell, touch, and taste even though these advancements require genetic alterations? The development of bionic eyes could help us see across great distances, view the world with night vision and infrared vision, and even see through walls. Synthetic hearing devices could help us hear the faintest of noises from far away and isolate sounds inside noisy areas such as concert halls. Ionic skin could help us detect changes in wind and air pressure, making it nearly impossible for someone to sneak up on us. Bionic smelling could help us locate people in almost any environment and identify substances in the air better than any animal. We could also identify the exact composition of the molecules in the air around us. Using bionic tastebuds, we could analyze the purity of water and identify the caloric composition of food just by tasting it. We could even perceive time much slower than usual, allowing us to have near-perfect reflexes and hyper-fast decision-making in life-or-death situations.[97] These developments certainly are appealing, but if they become possible, would individuals use them for the good of society?

Transhumanism and Telepathic Communication

The next advancement in transhumanism involves the use of telepathic communication. The concept involves developing a brain-computer interface that enables direct mind-to-mind communication. If this concept became reality, it would allow people to communicate with each other by simply thinking. This technology

---

[97] "Transhumanism: 20 Ways It Will Change the World," Future Business Tech, YouTube, https://www.youtube.com/watch?v=qcsihbGnXgE, accessed June 7, 2023.

would enable military personnel, employees, and even families to communicate with each other seamlessly. The suggested benefit of telepathic communication is that it would eliminate miscommunication and misunderstanding.

In 2014, researchers experimented with alleged brain-to-computer-to-brain communication. The research team established a binary code. Then, they attached electroencephalography sensors to the scalp. The sender moved either his hands or feet to indicate a 1 or a 0. The code then passed to the recipient over email. The receiver was blindfolded with a transcranial magnetic stimulation (TMS) system on his head. The TMS headset stimulated the recipient's brain, resulting in the person seeing flashes of light. A flash was equivalent to a "1" and a blank was a "0." From there, the code was translated back into text. It took about 70 minutes to relay the message. Though the methodology was quite cumbersome, the experiment proved successful. This basic technology set the stage for transhumanists to continue research toward one day facilitating actual brain-to-brain communication without the cumbersome equipment.[98]

In a more advanced stage, the technologies would enable people who speak different languages to communicate efficiently by converting their thoughts into a universal language that those with genetically enhanced brains could understand. If transhumanism developed to this level, privacy and personal security would cease to exist.[99]

Transhumanism and Neural Implants

Transhumanists would like to see researchers develop advanced neural (brain) implants that can receive knowledge downloaded directly through a high-speed internet connection with a large bandwidth. This technology would allow a person to possess a vast amount of information instantaneously, information that

---

[98] Corinne Iozzio, Scientists Prove That Telepathic Communication Is Within Reach, Smithsonian Magazine, October 2, 2014, https://www.smithsonianmag.com/innovation/scientists-prove-that-telepathic-communication-is-within-reach-180952868/, accessed August 23, 2023.

[99] "Transhumanism: 20 Ways It Will Change the World," Future Business Tech, YouTube, https://www.youtube.com/watch?v=qcsihbGnXgE, accessed June 7, 2023.

without the neural implant would have been beyond their ability to comprehend. The download could include information to perform skills that are linked with parts of the brain that perform motor control. In that way, the person could acquire, for example, the art of self-defense or the ability to excel in a sport or fly an airplane, in the amount of time it takes to complete the download to the neural implant.

Consider the impact of being able to learn the most difficult of subjects in a fraction of the time. The current educational system, including institutions of higher learning, would become obsolete, as the current educational formats would no longer be used.

Transhuman people would dominate in every area of life over people who had no genetic alterations or neural implants. Those possessing the technology would be able to access everything in digital format, including the vast amount information on the internet. There are AI systems currently in place that have trillions of data points gathered from the internet and other digital sources. AI could transfer its system contents instantaneously through a neural implant.[100] This scenario certainly seems beyond the realm of possibility. However, if only a fraction of this scenario comes to fruition, it has seismic implications.

Consider the horrific experiments that Nazi Germany conducted during the second world war.

> From 1933 to 1945, Nazi Germany carried out a campaign to "cleanse" German society of individuals viewed as biological threats to the nation's "health." The Nazis enlisted the help of physicians and medically trained geneticists, psychiatrists, and anthropologists to develop racial health policies. These policies began with the mass sterilization of many people in hospitals and other institutions and ended with the near annihilation of European Jewry.
>
> Unethical medical experimentation (without patient consent or any safeguards) carried out during the **Third Reich** may be divided into three categories.
>
> 1. Experiments dealing with the survival of military personnel
> 2. Experiments to test drugs and treatments

---

[100] Ibid.

3. Experiments to advance Nazi racial and ideological goals

The most infamous were the experiments of **Josef Mengele** on twins of all ages at Auschwitz. He also directed experiments on **Roma (Gypsies)**, as did Werner Fischer at Sachsenhausen, to determine how different "races" withstood various contagious diseases. The research of August Hirt at Strasbourg University also intended to establish "Jewish racial inferiority." Additional gruesome experiments meant to further Nazi racial goals included a series of sterilization experiments, undertaken primarily at Auschwitz and Ravensbrück. Scientists tested a number of methods in an effort to develop an efficient and inexpensive procedure for the mass sterilization of Jews, Roma, and other groups Nazi leaders considered to be racially or genetically undesirable.

The **Nuremberg Code** was created in the aftermath of the discovery of the camp experiments and subsequent trials to address abuses committed by medical professionals during the Holocaust. The Nuremberg Code included the principle of informed consent and required standards for research.[101]

History is replete with examples of what can happen when government officials use their power and influence for personal gain, to the detriment of the general populace. Dictators—past, present, and prophetic—have and will inflict profound suffering on millions of innocent and vulnerable people. The prophetic Scriptures guarantee that the powerful satanic global system during the Tribulation period will produce massive casualties. Those attempting to assist the one-world order will likely conduct unorthodox, dangerous experiments in their efforts to make transhumanism a reality. The only way to avoid becoming a victim of this terrifying scenario and escape the wrath of the Lord Jesus during the Tribulation period (should it commence in this generation) is to accept the gift of eternal life by faith in the Lord Jesus now (Eph. 2:8-9; 1 Thess. 5:9).

---

[101]United States Holocaust Memorial Museum, "Nazi Medical Experiments," Holocaust Encyclopedia, August 30, 2006, https://encyclopedia.ushmm.org/content/en/article/nazi-medical-experiments, accessed August 22, 2023.

Transhumanism and the Elimination of Disabilities

One of the great humanitarian goals of transhumanism is to treat disabilities. The eradication of deafness, blindness, the inability to speak, paralysis due to a severed spinal cord, and many other disabilities would be a marvelous achievement. The advancements would include the replacement of body parts and restoration of neural pathways, all of which, if achieved, would benefit humanity greatly.

The following expresses the sentiments of those wishing to see the advancement of transhumanism to abolish health issues that negatively impact human beings.

> Transhumanism is, at its root, a medical ideology, one promoting a technologically-mediated evolution that, according to the contemporary World Transhumanist Association (WTA), will enhance the mind, body, and psyche of the human being, taking the human body beyond its species-typical structure, function, and abilities. The WTA also defines the basic premise of transhumanism and, therefore, of transhumanist medicine: which is the belief that the present form of *Homo sapiens* does not represent the end of its development but a relatively nascent phase. GRIN—genetic, robotic, info, and nano-technologies will eventually artificially accelerate the natural evolutionary process, freeing the human being from the vagaries of random mutations and the incremental nature of variation and adaptation. As the Transhumanist Declaration states: "We favor morphological freedom—the right to modify and enhance one's body, cognition, and emotions."[102]

Where does appropriate medical care stop, and interference or ill-advised tampering begin? Those desiring to see progress for those suffering from physical abnormalities have proper intentions. However, when the very essence of a person is altered through

---

[102] Renée Mirkes, "Transhumanist Medicine: Can We Direct Its Power to the Service of Human Dignity?" March 29, 2019, Linacre Quarterly, https://www.ncbi.nlm.nih.gov/pmc/articles/PMC6537347/, accessed August 23, 2023.

genetic, robotic, info, and nano (GRIN) technologies, the treatment becomes suspect.

Does God's perfect plan for a person become altered by radical medical procedures? Will the Antichrist's one-world system seek to genetically alter humanity to gain control over his one-world government, economy, and religion? These questions should remain a serious topic of discussion as the disturbing words written by the apostle Paul to Timothy under the inspiration of the Holy Spirit become more relevant with each passing day.

> But know this, that in the last days perilous times will come: For men will be lovers of themselves, lovers of money, boasters, proud, blasphemers, disobedient to parents, unthankful, unholy, unloving, unforgiving, slanderers, without self-control, brutal, despisers of good, traitors, headstrong, haughty, lovers of pleasure rather than lovers of God, having a form of godliness but denying its power. And from such people turn away! (2 Tim. 3:1–5)

Transhumanism and Colonizing Other Planets

This particular goal of transhumanism lies within the realm of science fiction. However, far more research is required to determine if colonizing other planets makes any logical sense. Based on the seemingly bizarre nature of this goal, we will let the following quote speak for itself.

> As we begin to colonize Mars, Titan (the largest moon of Saturn), Europa (the Galilean moon of Jupiter), and Sirius (the largest star in the galaxy), we would need every advantage possible to survive in some of the harshest conditions imaginable. You could modify the human genome so that we can have increased resistance to radiation and the ability to thrive in low-gravity environments. These abilities would be essential to ensure that humans can build and maintain colonies on other planets in ways that robots may not be able to accomplish. Additionally, genetic engineering could help humans work at full speed for many hours at a time without getting tired. If humans that travel to other worlds are more machine than human that would lead to them being able to move heavy objects with ease and there

would be fewer ways to get seriously injured since machine parts would be easily replaceable.[103]

Developers, researchers, and technicians in the private and public sectors have vigorously worked on space travel for decades. Does God forbid domestic, international, or interplanetary air travel? The answer, based on all three forms of air travel being available, is obvious. The Scriptures do not address commercial space travel, so there appears to be no reason to stop its progress. However, the transhumanism scenario that suggests altering a human's ability to function and live in space remains debatable. The following summarizes the problem.

The question inevitably arises as to how a human being can become physically and psychologically fit for space travel and the colonization of new habitats. Can humans be optimized to sustain their health? <u>Transhumanists</u> specifically think about the optimization of humans. The explicit goals of the transhumanist vision are self-optimization, colonization of space, and immortality. The example of the recent Mars landing illustrates that a closer look at this vision has become relevant.

This post is not a plea for or against transhumanism. The term describes an eccentric and extreme vision of a technologically evolved human being, but not how to get there. The interesting discussion, in my view, is the examination of that very path and the questions it raises. This post aims to bring attention to the questions that arise in finding the path, not to evaluate the vision per se. We are already moving on this path, as the example of the Rover landing illustrates.[104]

Transhumanism and Resurrecting the Dead

---

[103] "Transhumanism: 20 Ways It Will Change the World," Future Business Tech, YouTube, https://www.youtube.com/watch?v=qcsihbGnXgE, accessed June 7, 2023.
[104] Gert Chriten, "Transhumanism – The technological evolution of humankind," GertChristen.org, March 31, 2021, https://www.gertchristen.org/transhumanism-rena-seiler/ accessed August 23, 2023.

God's design for human life for the past six thousand years is easy to follow. A person is born, they live a particular length of time, and then their body dies. This pattern is very simplistic but is nevertheless the only model known to humankind, barring divine intervention. That caveat implies the possibility of resurrection from the dead. God gave several individuals the power to miraculously raise people from the dead. Elijah raised the son of the widow of Zarephath from the dead (1 Kings17:17-24). Elisha raised a Shunamite's son from the dead (2 Kings 4:18-37). Jesus Himself raised Lazarus from the dead (John 11:38-39). Peter raised Tabitha, also known as Dorcas, from the dead (Acts 9:36-42). The apostle Paul raised Eutychus from the dead (Acts 20:7-12).

Therefore, the resurrection of the dead is certainly a biblical concept. However, would God allow the use of cryogenics, or other scientific means, to resurrect a person who has been dead for years? One of the major transhumanist goals is to obtain eternal life for the human body, or at least the human brain, by any means possible. The debate will continue on this issue, but from a strictly biblical perspective, the possibility of bodily resurrection apart from divine intervention is implausible.

Breakthroughs in fields such as cryogenics, brain preservation, and advanced life support systems could pave the way for reviving individuals declared clinically dead. The people who are choosing to cryogenically freeze their bodies might have their wishes fulfilled. They might wake up in a futuristic world that is totally different from the world of today. Perhaps people who have recently died could be resurrected as long as there isn't too much tissue damage. If there is tissue damage, the affected body parts could be replaced with mechanical and electronic parts. If that is not possible, perhaps we can make advances in brain preservation and focus on maintaining the integrity of neural connections and memories. Brains could be used decades from now to upload people's consciousness to computers and robots.[105]

---

[105] "Transhumanism: 20 Ways It Will Change the World," Future Business Tech, YouTube, https://www.youtube.com/watch?v=qcsihbGnXgE, accessed June 7, 2023.

Consider the field of cryonics, or cryogenics, which is the process of freezing a deceased person in the hopes that in the future, technology will advance to the point where all or parts of the body could be brought back to life and once again become useful. The following describes a company that is attempting to produce the desired outcomes of cryogenics.

> The company Alcor in the USA already offers the service (cryonics). The body is refrigerated directly after death has been determined and delivered to the company where they freeze the body (cryopreservation). In doing so, they use a very specialized process, because normal shock freezing would form ice crystals and thus damage the matter. You can choose whether you want to freeze only your head or your whole body. The goal is to thaw the body again in about 200 years and then to carry out a so-called "mind upload", i.e., to transfer consciousness into another body and thus let the person continue to live. However, since the technology for defrosting and mind uploading does not yet exist, the offer is based on the fact that this should be possible in about 200 years.[106]

In concluding the idea of bodily resurrection via transhumanist means, it is essential to know that God will resurrect all people from the dead to live eternally, either with Himself in heaven and eventually in the New Jerusalem (1 Cor. 15:50-54; 1 Thess. 4:13-18; Rev. 21:1-2), or in the disastrous place known as the lake of fire where the person will suffer constant torment forever (Dan. 12:1-2; Rev. 20:11-15; 21:8). Transhumanists appear to reject the biblical account of the guaranteed resurrection of the dead, and God's guarantee that all people will actually live for eternity. The failure of anyone to accept this biblical truth places them in a state of unbelief, which virtually guarantees a disastrous eternal outcome.

Jesus Christ, God's Son, provided the only means to enjoy eternal life. Jesus stated, "I am the way, the truth, and the life, no one comes unto the Father except by me" (John 14:6). Jesus, who is God, did not leave heaven's glory, come down to this earth in a human body, suffer the torture of crucifixion to the point of death, spend three days in the grave, and then experience the resurrection, for no reason. Jesus endured the entire process to provide the only means through which a human being can obtain eternal life with

---

[106]"Transhumanism – The Dream of Eternal Life," HWZ Digital, November 1, 2019, https://hwzdigital.ch/transhumanismus-der-traum-vom-ewigen-leben/, accessed August 23, 2023.

Him. Transhumanism cannot save anyone from eternal punishment, only faith in Jesus Christ can accomplish that eternal goal.

> For God so loved the world that He gave His only begotten Son, that whoever believes in Him should not perish but have everlasting life. For God did not send His Son into the world to condemn the world, but that the world through Him might be saved. (John 3:16–17).

> Moreover, brethren, I declare to you the gospel which I preached to you, which also you received and in which you stand, by which also you are saved, if you hold fast that word which I preached to you—unless you believed in vain. For I delivered to you first of all that which I also received: that Christ died for our sins according to the Scriptures, and that He was buried, and that He rose again the third day according to the Scriptures (1 Corinthians 15:1–4).

> For by grace you have been saved through faith, and that not of yourselves; it is the gift of God, not of works, lest anyone should boast. (Ephesians 2:8–9)

> If we receive the witness of men, the witness of God is greater; for this is the witness of God which He has testified of His Son. He who believes in the Son of God has the witness in himself; he who does not believe God has made Him a liar, because he has not believed the testimony that God has given of His Son. And this is the testimony: that God has given us eternal life, and this life is in His Son. He who has the Son has life; he who does not have the Son of God does not have life. These things I have written to you who believe in the name of the Son of God, that you may know that you have eternal life, and that you may continue to believe in the name of the Son of God. (1 John 5:9–13)

Transhumanism and Regenerative Medicine

The word "transhumanism" implies the use of science and technology to overcome human limitations and improve the human condition.

The word is composed of "trans" and "humanism". "Trans" in this context means "higher level through technology", and "humanism" means "better person". In other words, the transformation of the human being into a next higher level with the use of technology, a human being 2.0, so to speak. One does not want to try to overcome the human being, but to create a posthuman human through the human being. All transhumanists are united by the goal of optimizing the body and removing limitations. The basic idea behind it, to prolong life and overcome death, is not new, it has always existed and is deeply rooted in all of us.[107]

Although transhumanism is in its technical infancy when considering what its developers plan to achieve, integrating technology with medical procedures is not new.

The integration of technology into human beings has already been taking place as a matter of course for decades. In many cases, one does not question this integration. For example, when we speak of medical healing methods, we generally accept without questioning any technology applied to restore lost physical abilities (e.g., **artificial heart valves, organs, or limbs**). In the case of new methods, their justification is controversially discussed mainly in the beginning. Especially genetics, neurology, or embryology are considered sensitive topics. Altering DNA or neurological processes raises questions about long-term consequences that we cannot yet foresee, creating uncertainty and bringing central concepts into play: ethics and morality.[108]

---

[107] "Transhumanism – The Dream of Eternal Life," HWZ Digital, November 1, 2019, https://hwzdigital.ch/transhumanismus-der-traum-vom-ewigen-leben/, accessed August 23, 2023.

[108] Gert Chriten, "Transhumanism – The technological evolution of humankind," GertChristen.org, March 31, 2021,

The concept of regenerative medicine, or regenerative medical procedures, describes what must take place to morph a human into a transhuman. "Transhumanists envision a future where humans transcend biological limitations, such as mortality, frailty, and susceptibility to diseases. They argue that through technology, we can augment our bodies and minds, achieving a new level of existence known as "post-humanity."109 Everything mentioned in the last statement has an undeniable medical nexus. In addition, "transhumanists aim to slow down, halt, or even reverse aging. This would not only extend the human lifespan but also improve health and vitality in old age. Techniques such as gene editing, telomere extension, or regenerative medicine could play crucial roles in this."110

When considering the implementation of regenerative medicine, "the Salk Institute and the Weizmann Institute are also working on ways to regenerate people who are approaching old age. Another company, BioViva, is using gene-editing technology to lengthen the telomeres at the end of chromosomes and thus surpass the Hayflick Limit (forty to sixty normal human cell population divisions) defying cellular senescence and aging."[111] For those outside the medical field, these concepts may be difficult to understand, but the underlying issue is that regenerative medicine is definitely part of the plan for accomplishing the transhumanist agenda.

Consider the following thought-provoking suggestions regarding what transhumanism could achieve through medical advancements, including regenerative medicine.

> Humans could heal more rapidly by leveraging cutting-edge developments in fields such as regenerative medicine, nanotechnology, and bioengineering. Scientists could create

---

https://www.gertchristen.org/transhumanism-rena-seiler/ accessed August 23, 2023.

[109] Transhumanism: Merging Humans and Technology, June 25, 2023, Mirage News, https://www.miragenews.com/transhumanism-merging-humans-and-technology-1033779/,Accessed August 23, 2023.

[110] Ibid.

[111] Renée Mirkes, "Transhumanist Medicine: Can We Direct Its Power to the Service of Human Dignity?" March 29, 2019, Linacre Quarterly, https://www.ncbi.nlm.nih.gov/pmc/articles/PMC6537347/, accessed August 23, 2023.

advanced therapies and interventions that dramatically accelerate the body's natural healing processes. We may even gain the capability to regenerate lost limbs. Specifically, we could harness the power of stem cells, growth factors, and gene-editing techniques to stimulate the repair and regeneration of damaged tissues. Nanobots could be programmed to perform targeted repairs at the cellular level repairing damaged tissues with remarkable precision and efficiency. This healing capability would help improve the prospects for patients with severe injuries, chronic conditions, and life-threatening illnesses. As the level of technological advancement becomes greater, the healing process could become exponentially faster. This could potentially be one of the many mind-blowing capabilities enabled by fully developed super intelligent AIs.[112]

There are many concerns when considering the goals and methodologies in the quest for transhumanism. "For instance, we are still in the early stages of understanding the human brain's complexity, and attempts to augment or modify it could have unforeseen consequences."[113] The concept of regenerative medicine raises moral, ethical, spiritual, and technical concerns. However, based on the high interest in transhumanism and the significant resources already invested in its development, it appears to be here to stay.

Transhumanism and Creativity

One of the less caustic topics in transhumanism is the area of entertainment and creativity. The entertainment industry is massive, with the average household spending almost $3,000 a year on home entertainment.[114] Transhumanism desires to develop an entirely

---

[112] "Transhumanism: 20 Ways It Will Change the World," Future Business Tech, YouTube, https://www.youtube.com/watch?v=qcsihbGnXgE, accessed June 7, 2023.

[113] Transhumanism: Merging Humans and Technology, June 25, 2023, Mirage News, https://www.miragenews.com/transhumanism-merging-humans-and-technology-1033779/, Accessed August 23, 2023.

[114] Lindsay Bishop, Average Household Budget: How Much Does the Typical American Spend? November 28, 2022,

new model for entertainment, whereby the individual has the capacity to create their own entertainment, which far exceeds the concept of daydreaming.

Creativity would be at an all-time high as humans integrate their minds more and more with AI and computers. The level of creativity in the world would exponentially increase. It could lead to entirely new forms of art and entertainment. Humans could gain the ability to imagine movies in their minds, have AIs enhanced as movies, and then telepathically share those movies with millions of other people, all within the span of one minute. We could reach a point where we create entire VR *(virtual reality)* worlds using our thought patterns. We could invite our friends to those worlds, and we could choose any elements of those two worlds instantaneously. We could even merge multiple human minds into one digital entity that can imagine things that even AIs have trouble imagining.[115]

Creativity in the entertainment and cultural areas of society appears benign on its face. However, when considering the transhumanist methodology to not only create new art, movies, and other forms of entertainment but to also transfer those creative ideas to others through the development of brain-to-brain communication, the idea becomes a matter of significant concern on multiple levels.

Transhumanism and Cybercrime

Transhumanism would enable new forms of crime that would pose an extremely difficult challenge to law enforcement. Transhuman cyber criminals could brain-hack unsuspecting victims. This could entail the cyber-criminal, in its simplest form, eavesdropping on another person's thoughts. In a more advanced stage, the invasive criminal could control their victim's thoughts, erase their memory, and even control their body movements. In

---

https://www.valuepenguin.com/average-household-budget#:~:text=The%20average%20American%20household%20spends%20%242%2C912%20per%20year%20on%20entertainment, accessed August 24, 2023.

[115] "Transhumanism: 20 Ways It Will Change the World," Future Business Tech, YouTube, https://www.youtube.com/watch?v=qcsihbGnXgE, accessed June 7, 2023

some cases, this could lead to the theft of intellectual property, among other undesirable outcomes.

Consider the following information that provides a broad scope of what the transhumanist cyber-criminal could perform.

The existence of cyborgs, that is, humans who are part machine and part human is an imminent reality, and brings to light enemies known in the cyber world, but which previously had a low capacity to reach life in the material world. Cyber threats such as malware, DDoS attacks, among others, have an unreachable ability to affect the physical security of human beings, from accidents to more serious events that can bring some bodily, psychological, and fatal injury. Imagine, in a hypothetical situation, the possibility of cracking a pacemaker, and making the victim a hostage of this crime that occurs both in the virtual and physical world.

It may seem surreal to be able to lead the victim to death. But, when comparing a crime of physical and virtual homicide, a cybercriminal has fewer restrictions when committing the act, as he has no physical contact with the victim, in addition to reducing his exposure and level of aggression as a criminal, since the latter does not need to use a weapon to commit the offense.

Although this scenario is a mere fiction in today's world, when comparing the incidence of virtual and physical crimes, the hypothetical situation mentioned does not seem so surreal. For example, it is enough to assess the crimes of theft, extortion, fraud, and others that are committed through the use of personal data, even though there are laws that punish this type of attitude, as well as technologies such as reputation monitoring or VIP monitoring, which allow identifying whether the monitored data has been breached in the cyber world.

Certainly, innovation is essential for the improvement and evolution of life, and especially for one of humanity's dreams, which is immortality through transhumanism. But, without the proper security controls that allow us to transcend between the physical and virtual world, this reality can become humanity's nightmare which is extinction.[116]

The broad scope of criminal and suspect activities the nefarious transhumanist could perform is very concerning. The potential for people with robotic arms and legs with super strength to cause harm to others is a genuine possibility. The current level of violence in America and around the world is already at a horrific stage. The massive number of weapons held by private citizens, organizations, and the government already account for a significant number of murders and so-called justified killings. If transhumanism develops the superhuman body, the propensity for increased violence is a very real possibility. Society would need law enforcement that is exponentially more advanced and powerful to deal with these additional threats in society.

Concluding Remarks

The following is an excellent summary of the issues posed by the continued development and implementation of transhumanism. Transhumanism stands at the intersection of science, technology, and philosophy, challenging our understanding of what it means to be human. While it promises potentially revolutionary benefits, it also poses profound ethical and societal questions. As we stand on the brink of a future where technology and humanity may become ever more closely entwined, the debates and discussions around transhumanism are likely to become increasingly important in shaping that future.[117]

Transhumanism combined with artificial intelligence, if developed as the research suggests, provides the potential for marvelous benefits to society. If, on the other hand, those with evil intent use the advancement in transhumanist and AI technology for

---

[116] Silas Queiroz, "The Cybersecurity In The Age Of Transhumanism" August 2, 2021, Linkedin, https://www.linkedin.com/pulse/cybersecurity-age-transhumanism-silas-queiroz, , accessed August 23, 2023.

[117] "Transhumanism: Merging Humans and Technology," June 25, 2023, Mirage News, https://www.miragenews.com/transhumanism-merging-humans-and-technology-1033779/,Accessed August 23, 2023.

narcissistic endeavors, it is guaranteed to have severely negative repercussions.

The Scriptures vividly describe prophecies that God will bring to complete fulfillment, which very well could involve the use of AI and transhumanism. The caution is for all people to consider in real-time the technology that developers are rapidly forming on the domestic and world stage, and to guard themselves against the potential deception and associated negative outcomes. God Himself often warns people through the Scriptures to guard themselves against deception and temptations that will lead to a disastrous end.

When Jesus sent out His disciples to spread the good news about His coming, He warned them as follows.

> Behold, I send you out as sheep in the midst of wolves. Therefore, be wise as serpents and harmless as doves. But beware of men, for they will deliver you up to councils and scourge you in their synagogues. You will be brought before governors and kings for My sake, as a testimony to them and to the Gentiles. But when they deliver you up, do not worry about how or what you should speak. For it will be given to you in that hour what you should speak; for it is not you who speak, but the Spirit of your Father who speaks in you.
>
> Now brother will deliver up brother to death, and a father his child; and children will rise up against parents and cause them to be put to death. And you will be hated by all for My name's sake. But he who endures to the end will be saved. When they persecute you in this city, flee to another. For assuredly, I say to you, you will not have gone through the cities of Israel before the Son of Man comes. (Matt. 10:16–23)

The apostle Paul warns the current generation, "Now the Spirit expressly says that in latter times some will depart from the faith, giving heed to deceiving spirits and doctrines of demons, speaking lies in hypocrisy, having their own conscience seared with a hot iron" (1 Tim. 4:1–2). He further warns, "Therefore, let him who thinks he stands take heed lest he fall. No temptation has overtaken you except such as is common to man; but God is faithful, who will not allow you to be tempted beyond what you are able, but with the temptation will also make the way of escape, that you may be able to bear it" (1 Cor. 10:12–13).

America and rest of the world are in a very precarious position. Government leaders are constantly looking for ways to make themselves more powerful. Corporations must continually look at the most advanced technology to remain competitive in a global market. Many of the ultra-rich desire to find the magic formula that guarantees their longevity. Satan desires to defeat God's perfect will for all people, and he is continually working towards that end. The charge of God is to exercise discernment, reject that which is evil, and embrace that which is honoring to the Lord.

Here we stand; we cannot, we must not be moved!

CHAPTER SIX
The De-Evolution of Democracy

On November 2, 2022, President Joseph Biden gave a passionate speech that focused on the preservation of democracy in the United States of America.[118] The President spoke before the mid-term elections, with the apparent goal of moving people to reject any candidate who held to the political positions of the "MAGA Republicans," specifically those who aligned themselves with former President Donald Trump. The speech presented a picture of the loss of democracy facing America if its citizens cast ballots for those whom he considered the wrong candidates. According to Biden, voting conservative Republications into office during the mid-term elections constituted the downfall of democracy. Many conservatives and liberals were deeply moved by the piercing words of that very pointed speech. News commentators across the country and around the world dissected the speech and were divided in their assessment.

Biden's speech forced many people to consider, if not research, his claims. In his opinion, the results of the mid-term election held serious consequences for America if the "wrong" outcome occurred. The President's concerning words sparked many questions. What is the meaning of democracy, specifically as it applies to the United States of America? How could one election potentially destroy democracy? What are the principles, policies, and results of a properly functioning democracy? What were the positive and negative outcomes when comparing President Biden's administration with President Trump's? Answering those questions will help us ascertain whether the downfall of American democracy was even possible at that point. Careful examination of empirical data and factual unspun research should balance our evaluation of these issues rather than simply accepting the statements of a politically motivated speaker relying on emotionally charged rhetoric.

Based on the federal government's performance in various areas over the past seven years (2016-2022), there is indeed a real concern regarding the state of the Union and where it is currently heading. President Trump's administration was decisively

---

[S]See Appendix D for the full transcript of President Biden's speech from November 2, 2023.

nationalist, focused on "Make America Great Again." His administration advocated for a strong, self-sufficient America that bowed the knee to no other country. Yet he attempted to work with other countries within reason to maintain peaceful relations. Biden's administration holds a strong globalist perspective, which emphasizes issues that require global cooperation, such as response to pandemics, general health care, climate change, international travel, the economy, technological advancements, energy, and other concerns important to every country. America's voters must decide if nationalism or globalism should constitute America's future direction.

Considering the development of artificial intelligence (AI) and transhumanism, the question arises as to how current and future governments will use these technologies. AI presents more of an immediate concern for America and other countries that are actively using it, whereas the development of transhumanism is still in its infancy. We have already discussed many positive outcomes from AI. However, there are also pressing concerns regarding how governments, corporations, and individuals have and are using AI technology. The improper use of AI could increase the propensity toward the de-evolution of democracy.

President Biden's impassioned speech on the potential danger to democracy, specifically if the voters do not vote the right candidates into office, gave pause to all people—conservatives, liberals, and moderates—as to what in the world is happening in America. What is a democracy? What is a republic? Will America forsake the Constitutional principles on which the founding fathers formed the country? Will America stand on the Constitution and the rule of law, or will it deteriorate into a socialist, Marxist, communist, dictator-run country? Is *the de-evolution of democracy* currently taking place, and if the answer is yes, how are AI and potentially transhumanism playing a part?

Biden's powerful words opened the discussion regarding *the de-evolution of democracy*. This chapter will critically examine that concept as it fits into the biblical prophetic scenario. In the Scriptures, God provided His unalterable prophetic plan, which includes a precise timetable of events. The Bible never mentions the United States of America in any prophecy, which is extremely concerning. Therefore, based on that fact, what does the future hold for America and the millions of people who call America home? Will the potential de-evolution of democracy end in tragedy? Only time will tell.

Democracy Defined

In light of Biden's speech, it becomes necessary to understand what is meant by democracy. Merriam-Webster states, "The word *democracy* most often refers to a form of government in which people choose leaders by voting."[119] That very simplistic definition leads to the question, what is a democratic system of government, which **Merriam-Webster** defines as "a form of government in which supreme power is vested in the people and exercised by them directly or indirectly through a system of representation usually involving periodic free elections."[120]

There is considerable debate regarding whether America is a democracy or a republic. On that issue, **Merriam-Webster** provides the following commentary.

> Is the United States a democracy or a republic? The United States is both a democracy and a republic. Democracies and republics are both forms of government in which supreme power resides in the citizens. The word *republic* refers specifically to a government in which those citizens elect representatives who govern according to the law. The word *democracy* can refer to this same kind of representational government, or it can refer instead to what is also called a *direct democracy*, in which the citizens themselves participate in the act of governing directly.[121]

The following explanation delves further into the differences between a democracy and a republic, and which is more accurate in describing America's government.

> Is the United States a *democracy* or a *republic*? This is one of those "either/or" questions that seems like it should

---

[119]"Democracy." MERRIAM-WEBSTER.COM DICTIONARY, Merriam-Webster, https://www.merriam-webster.com/dictionary/democracy. Accessed 24 Aug. 2023.
[120] Ibid.
[121] Ibid.

have a straightforward answer; after all, two such different words must have two different definitions, right?

The short answer is that *democracy* and *republic* are frequently used to mean the same thing: a government in which the people vote for their leaders. This was the important distinction at the time of the founding of the United States, in direct contrast with the rule of a king, or monarchy, in Great Britain. In part because that context was clear to everyone involved in the American Revolution, these terms were used interchangeably in the late 1700s.

Both *democracy* and *republic* meant that the power to govern was held by the people rather than a monarch.

At the same time, it is true that there is nuance and difference between these words, according to their historical use and etymology: *democracy* comes from the Greek roots meaning "rule by the people," and the most basic understanding of the word's original meaning refers to the direct democracy of ancient Greece.

Republic comes from the Latin roots meaning "public good" or "public affair," used in ancient Rome to mean simply "state" or "country" with reference to the representative democracy of the Roman Republic. The elected representatives in Congress are a contemporary example of this kind of government.

Because *democracy* is an abstract name for a system and *republic* is the more concrete result of that system, *democracy* is frequently used when the emphasis is on the system itself. We could say that *democracy* is to *republic* as *monarchy* is to *kingdom*.

These terms are not mentioned in the Declaration of Independence, a document that nevertheless expresses clearly that governments should be established "deriving their just powers from the consent of the governed." This reads like a definition of both *democracy* and *republic*. In Article IV Section V of the Constitution, the term *republican* is used as an adjective: "The United States shall guarantee to every State in this Union a Republican Form of Government."

In the final analysis, what these words share in meaning is much more important than how they differ.[122]

Republicans, Democrats, libertarians, independents, and all other political parties should desire elections free from corruption and manipulation. Several politicians, both Democrats and Republicans, have voiced their opinions regarding election fraud in the past decade.[123] "One may argue that the trend of treating opposing-party presidents, even rhetorically, as cheaters-in-chief has been bad for the country and toxic for our politics. Perhaps, sooner or later, this trend was inevitably going to escalate into active efforts to overturn election results one doesn't like—i.e., a de facto negation of democracy."[124]

Aaron Blake wrote the following in an article published by the Washington Post.

But Trump isn't the only one going down this road right now. Republicans have increasingly warned that Democrats will "steal" Florida. Sen. Marco Rubio (R-Fla.) has tweeted that "democrat lawyers plan to steal [the] #Florida election." Florida Republican Gov. Rick Scott's adviser has said Scott won't lose to Sen. Bill Nelson (D-Fla.) "unless they steal it from him in court."

And now even some big-name Democrats are using similar language, alleging that the Georgia governor's race will be "stolen" from them, too. Sen. Cory Booker (D-N.J.) has said the "election is being stolen from" Democrat Stacey Abrams. Hillary Clinton has said Abrams would have won "if she'd had a fair election." And on Wednesday, Sen. Sherrod

---

[122] "Democracy or Republic: What's the difference?" MERRIAM-WEBSTER.COM DICTIONARY, Merriam-Webster, https://www.merriam-webster.com/grammar/democracy-and-republic, accessed August 25, 2023.

[123] Donald Trump, Hillary Clinton, Stacey Abrams, Al Gore, Jimmy Carter, Are All Cited As Having Made Comments Regarding Election Fraud. "Yes, Democrats Have Called Some Elections Illegitimate. "GOP Election Denialism Is Far Worse." CATO Institute, November 8, 2022, https://www.cato.org/commentary/yes-democrats-have-called-some-elections-illegitimate-gop-election-denialism-far-worse, accessed August 25, 2023.

[124] Ibid.

Brown (D-Ohio) went so far as to say, "If Stacey Abrams doesn't win in Georgia, they stole it."[125]

Many open-source news stories are available to document claims from a diverse sector of politicians regarding election corruption and fraud. The issue is not confined to the United States of America but is an issue on an international scale. The purpose of this chapter is not to point out issues in voter integrity, but to show how current events are setting the stage for God to fulfill Bible prophecy.

The Scriptures clearly state that during the Tribulation, mass corruption will occur on a global scale. The future satanic global system, led by the Antichrist and the false prophet, does not allow for a republic or a representative democracy. The dictator-run government, economy, and religion will not require any elections, as those who refuse to comply and submit to the dictates of the Antichrist will face execution (Rev. 13:15).

How will government leaders during the Tribulation know which people are complying? We return to the most important piece of the biblical narrative to reinforce how Satan intends to enforce compliance.

> He was granted power to give breath to the image of the beast, that the image of the beast should both speak and cause as many as would not worship the image of the beast to be killed. He causes all, both small and great, rich and poor, free and slave, to receive a mark on their right hand or on their foreheads, and that no one may buy or sell except one who has the mark or the name of the beast, or the number of his name. Here is wisdom. Let him who has understanding calculate the number of the beast, for it is the number of a man: His number is 666. (Rev. 13:15–18)

America has been subject to the de-evolution of democracy for quite some time. The founders of America established the Constitution and its Amendments to guide all future leaders in the honorable preservation of the United States of America. The

---

[125] Aaron Blake, "Democrats Are Now Going There On 'Stolen' Elections," The Washington Post, November 15, 2018, https://www.washingtonpost.com/politics/2018/11/15/democrats-are-now-going-there-stolen-elections/, accessed August 25, 2023.

Preamble of the Constitution sets the tone for this historic document.

> We the People of the United States, in Order to form a more perfect Union, establish Justice, insure domestic Tranquility, provide for the common defense, promote the general Welfare, and secure the Blessings of Liberty to ourselves and our Posterity, do ordain and establish this Constitution for the United States of America.[126]

The First Amendment to the Constitution is of utmost importance to all citizens of the United States of America.

> Congress shall make no law respecting an establishment of religion, or prohibiting the free exercise thereof; or abridging the freedom of speech, or of the press; or the right of the people peaceably to assemble, and to petition the Government for a redress of grievances.[127]

Every person must have the freedoms expressed in the First Amendment of the Constitution. Freedom of speech, freedom to peaceably assemble, and freedom of religion are the absolute mandates for the country to live free from socialism, Marxism, communism, tyranny, and dictatorship. When the people believe the government falls outside the Constitution, and the powerful leadership diminishes their First Amendment rights, disunity and even chaos can materialize, as witnessed throughout past and recent history. The very crux of the issue is the de-evolution of democracy.

What do the political leaders domestically and internationally want to accomplish? How many political leaders in powerful countries desire to move away from autonomous leadership to a global system? How many countries want the World Health Organization (WHO), the World Economic Forum (WEF), and other global groups to dictate global health care, finances, energy sources and consumption, alleged climate issues, and other major areas concerning to the world's populace? How many countries literally desire to hand over their country's sovereignty to a global organization led by a global dictator? The amazing truth is that

---

[126] "U.S. Constitution | Constitution Annotated | Congress.gov | Library of Congress," https://constitution.congress.gov/constitution/preamble/, accessed August 26, 2023.
[127] Ibid.

scenario is exactly what will come to fruition according to Bible prophecy. The de-evolution of democracy is a worldwide issue, which Scripture guarantees will end with the abolition of democracy.

The important issue for the current generation regards how many Constitutional freedoms and rule-of-law protections will face denigration as the de-evolution of democracy continues. How many churches will agencies shut down because they refuse to voluntarily close their doors when the government institutes a health-hazard emergency? How many parents, who refuse to allow their children to go to a school where their children are forced to hear about gender identity, puberty suppression, hormone therapy, transgender surgery, and sexual experimentation will be labeled domestic terrorists and face potential prosecution? How many domestic and international flights will the governments of the world cancel based on a stated crisis? How will people survive if officials shut down the power grids based on saving energy and the climate? What happens to the food supply if governments continue the significant reduction of livestock, based on animal waste allegedly harming the environment? What happens to countries when borders are opened, allowing criminals, dissidents, extremists, and those seeking to overtake a country to walk across the border uninhibited? What happens if, as many have stated on both sides of the political aisle, elections, which are one of the defining functions of a democracy, are infiltrated by nefarious individuals, and reverse the will of the people by undercover, massively resourced people and organizations? Is it any wonder why civilizations collapse, empires are conquered, countries become impotent, and people become slaves to corrupt leadership? The absolute, unalterable truth is found in the Scriptures.

How many people will the judicial system charge with a hate crime for simply stating their objections to the cancel culture, woke policies, alleged social injustices, and other liberal-led mandates? All these issues are setting the stage for the prophetic scenario, where everyone's preferences and convictions will be subject to the new rule of law, which will mandate that one either worship the worldwide leader, follow his economic plan, and obey the laws of his government, or face almost certain execution. Is it any wonder why the alarm is deafening when observing the rapid development in AI, transhumanism, and the de-evolution of democracy?

The apostle Paul reveals why the de-evolution of democracy and the eventual collapse of the American government and every other government in the world will occur.

> But we have renounced the hidden things of shame, not walking in craftiness nor handling the word of God deceitfully, but by manifestation of the truth commending ourselves to every man's conscience in the sight of God. But even if our gospel is veiled, it is veiled to those who are perishing, whose minds the god of this age has blinded, who do not believe, lest the light of the gospel of the glory of Christ, who is the image of God, should shine on them. (2 Cor. 4:2–4)

The god of this world, Satan, whom the one and only true God allows to run his diabolical system, will form the one-world government, economy, and religion, destroying any semblance of democracy on a global scale. Consider the following politically charged question posed by many conservatives in the past few years. Why did God allow someone into the Oval Office who is moving the country in a direction that opposes so many of the country's conservative values? There is one answer that appears to be the reason why God Himself allowed the leadership in America to move in a direction that conservatives and most Christians find deplorable. Consider the following: President Trump's campaign slogan, *Make America Great Again,* resounded with nationalism. Trump was all about America's strength and prosperity. President Biden embraces a different perspective on America's place on the world stage. Globalism seems to have the attention of the current Administration, more than making America stand out as a superpower. The biblical prophetic scenario requires that eventually, the world will bow the knee to the one-world dictator or face execution. Is it possible that the Lord is ready to move the world towards His prophetic plan's fulfillment, and is putting the leadership in place that will embrace the leadership of the one-world dictator, the Antichrist? God did not tell us when the Rapture would occur. However, it is absolutely amazing that what is happening around the world and in America is preparing the platform for the prophesied one-world system.

As people begin to understand the catastrophic consequences of the de-evolution of democracy, the prayer is that they will desire to understand why this issue is taking place. Instead of simply going through life hoping for a good future, it is imperative that each person instead, turn to the only Book that has documented proof of 500 prophecies coming to fulfillment, the Bible. Everyone must realize that their only hope for their immediate and long-term future is to receive the gift of eternal life by placing their faith in the death, burial, and resurrection of Jesus Christ, who personally paid the complete penalty for their sin.

> But when the kindness and the love of God our Savior toward man appeared, not by works of righteousness which we have done, but according to His mercy He saved us, through the washing of regeneration and renewing of the Holy Spirit, whom He poured out on us abundantly through Jesus Christ our Savior, that having been justified by His grace we should become heirs according to the hope of eternal life (Titus 3:4-7).

Receiving Jesus Christ as one's personal Savior does not guarantee a life free of trials. What placing one's faith in Jesus does accomplish is providing believers with guidance, and the love of the Lord, and guaranteeing all believers eternity in His presence.

> If we receive the witness of men, the witness of God is greater; for this is the witness of God which He has testified of His Son. He who believes in the Son of God has the witness in himself; he who does not believe God has made Him a liar, because he has not believed the testimony that God has given of His Son. And this is the testimony: that God has given us eternal life, and this life is in His Son. He who has the Son has life; he who does not have the Son of God does not have life. These things I have written to you who believe in the name of the Son of God, that you may know that you have eternal life, and that you may continue to believe in the name of the Son of God. (1 John 5:9–13)

Dictatorship

The focus of this book is examining the biblical prophetic scenario regarding the guaranteed formation of the one-world satanically run system, and revealing some of the newest tools, such as AI, transhumanism, and the de-evolution of democracy that Satan, the Antichrist, and the false prophet will use to control the one-world government, economy, and religion. Therefore, understanding the significant amount of biblical content regarding the satanic trinity will help one comprehend why current events are setting the stage for God to fulfill His prophetic word, as found in the Scriptures.

The Descriptive Origin of the Antichrist

There are only four times the word antichrist is found in the Bible, and only one specifically refers to the title of the coming one-world ruler. The prefix *anti* can also mean *instead of* and both meanings will apply to this coming world leader. He will overtly oppose Christ and at the same time, pass himself off as Christ. He will be the most powerful dictator the world has ever seen, making Caesar, Hitler, Mao, and Saddam seem tame in comparison.

The first time John uses the word *Antichrist*, he is directly referring to the prophetic personage of the satanically charged one-world ruler. "Little children, it is the last hour; and as you have heard that the Antichrist is coming, even now many antichrists have come, by which we know that it is the last hour" (1 John 2:18). False teachers came into the church and tried to tempt genuine Christians to abandon the faith (1 John 2:19). These teachers caused some to doubt their faith, so John wrote the passage, under the inspiration of the Holy Spirit (2 Tim. 3:16) to correct the errors of these teachers by giving three tests to determine the authenticity of our faith. The tests included, did they believe in the Incarnation of Jesus Christ, did they practice holy living, and finally did they love others (1 John 1:1-5). Therefore, if someone denies the Incarnation and that Jesus is the Son of God, then they have the spirit of the antichrist (1 John 2:18-25).

John used the word antichrist a second time in 1 John 2:22: "Who is a liar but he who denies that Jesus is the Christ? He is antichrist who denies the Father and the Son." This first reference to the concept of antichrist is a general word used to describe anyone who denies Jesus is God, or more specifically the Messiah, which is the meaning associated with the word *Christ*.

The apostle John wrote this verse to combat a heresy that occurred when Cerinthus taught that Jesus was the Christ but denied the apostolic meaning of the title. Followers of Cerinthus rejected biblical orthodoxy by claiming that Jesus was a mere man and that He was not God Incarnate. The heresy claimed that Jesus only possessed the spirit of Christ, thus denying that Jesus was the Christ.[128] John further documents the truth that Jesus is the Christ as

---

[128] Matt Slick, What is Cerinthianism? CARM, June 18, 2014, https://carm.org/about-heresies/what-is-cerinthianism/, accessed August 26, 2023.

he personally witnessed. "That which was from the beginning, which we have heard, which we have seen with our eyes, which we have looked upon, and our hands have handled, concerning the Word of life-- the life was manifested, and we have seen, and bear witness, and declare to you that eternal life which was with the Father and was manifested to us" (1 John 1:1-2).

The third time John uses the word Antichrist is in 1 John 4:2-4. "By this you know the Spirit of God: Every spirit that confesses that Jesus Christ has come in the flesh is of God, and every spirit that does not confess that Jesus Christ has come in the flesh is not of God. And this is the *spirit* of the Antichrist, which you have heard was coming, and is now already in the world. You are of God, little children, and have overcome them, because He who is in you is greater than he who is in the world." This is the second of two times where the word Antichrist refers to the prophetic one-world ruler. However, John is not talking in context about the future Antichrist, but the current anti-Christ attitude that has and continues to exist in the world. John states that the spirit, or attitude and practice, of the Antichrist were permeating society back during the first century. The Antichrist did not exist in bodily form during John's lifetime, but the satanic attitude, which is anti-Christ, has been alive since Satan rebelled against God in the Garden of Eden (Gen. 3; Isa. 14:12-17; Ez. 28).

The apostle John finally uses the term antichrist in 2 John 1:7. "For many deceivers have gone out into the world who do not confess Jesus Christ *as* coming in the flesh. This is a deceiver and an antichrist." Once again, John uses a broad-brush approach in using the term *antichrist.* Those who choose to deny the deity of the Lord Jesus Christ and propagate a false gospel or false religion, fall under the definition of an antichrist. In the Gospel of John, he confirms the deceptive practices of Satan.

> Jesus said to them, "If God were your Father, you would love Me, for I proceeded forth and came from God; nor have I come of Myself, but He sent Me. Why do you not understand My speech? Because you are not able to listen to My word. You are of your father the devil, and the desires of your father you want to do. He was a murderer from the beginning, and does not stand in the truth, because there is no truth in him. When he speaks a lie, he speaks from his own resources, for he is a liar and the father of it. But because I tell the truth, you do not believe Me. (John 8:42–45)

The Dominant Arrival of the Antichrist
The Scriptures discuss the coming of the Antichrist in multiple passages, most prominently in the prophecies of Daniel 2, 7, and Revelation 13. Daniel and the apostle John vividly describe the scope and power of the one-world ruler. The Antichrist will perform a multitude of atrocities during his short seven-year reign. Daniel described the unfolding of the satanic empire when God revealed the interpretation of King Nebuchadnezzar's dream.

The king of Babylon, King Nebuchadnezzar, had a dream that included a statue of multiple metals. "This image's head was of fine gold, its chest and arms of silver, its belly and thighs of bronze, its legs of iron, its feet partly of iron and partly of clay" (Dan. 2:32-33). Each section of the image represented a succeeding and more powerful empire, as Daniel brings to light. The kingdom that existed when Daniel wrote his book was Babylon. "You, O king, are a king of kings. For the God of heaven has given you a kingdom, power, strength, and glory; and wherever the children of men dwell, or the beasts of the field and the birds of the heaven, He has given them into your hand, and has made you ruler over them all—you are this head of gold" (Dan 2:37-38). The second kingdom, which had not yet come to power when Daniel wrote, was Medo-Persia; the third kingdom was Greece, and the fourth was Rome. "But after you shall arise another kingdom *(Medo-Persia)* inferior to yours; then another, a third kingdom of bronze *(Greece)*, which shall rule over all the earth. And the fourth kingdom shall be as strong as iron *(Rome)*, inasmuch as iron breaks in pieces and shatters everything; and like iron that crushes, that kingdom will break in pieces and crush all the others" (Daniel 2:39-40). Daniel's prophecy, through verse 40, came to complete fulfilment.

Daniel's prophecy, starting in verse 41, remains unfulfilled. However, God will bring this startling prophecy to fulfillment, just as He has fulfilled every other prophecy, with extreme exactness. The next section of his prophecy refers to the future kingdom, where Antichrist will rule. Daniel reveals, "Whereas you saw the feet and toes, partly of potter's clay and partly of iron, the kingdom shall be divided; yet the strength of the iron shall be in it, just as you saw the iron mixed with ceramic clay. And as the toes of the feet were partly of iron and partly of clay, so the kingdom shall be partly strong and partly fragile. As you saw iron mixed with ceramic clay, they will mingle with the seed of men; but they will not adhere to one another, just as iron does not mix with clay" (Dan. 2:41-43).

Daniel's prophecy speaks to the formation of what theologians call the *Revived Roman Empire*. The toes on the image are partly of iron, which we know from history represents Rome, or the fourth empire prophesied by Daniel, and then clay, which represents, at a minimum, ten confederate nations who align with the Antichrist. Daniel 2 does not address the one-world ruler, but Daniel 7, a companion passage, does discuss the Antichrist, who is called *the little horn* or the one rising amidst ten horns, symbolizing the ten confederate nations (Dan. 7:8).

Daniel 7 discusses the same subject as Daniel 2 but with a different symbolic scenario. In Chapter 7, Daniel describes four beasts, whereas in Chapter 2, Daniel describes the large image or statue made up of four different metals. The first three beasts represent Babylon, Medo Persia, and Greece (Dan. 7:17). The fourth beast represents the past Rome empire, and the horns and crowns on the fourth beast's head symbolically refer to the future Revived Roman Empire, which Antichrist will rule.

> Then I wished to know the truth about the fourth beast *(Rome)*, which was different from all the others, exceedingly dreadful, with its teeth of iron and its nails of bronze, which devoured, broke in pieces, and trampled the residue with its feet; and the ten horns that were on its head *(Revived Roman Empire)*, and the other horn *(Antichrist)* which came up, before which three fell *(three of the ten nations that originally give their allegiance to Antichrist will be destroyed)*, namely, that horn which had eyes and a mouth which spoke pompous words, whose appearance was greater than his fellows. (Dan. 7:19-20)

Dwight Pentecost, one of the great scholars on the doctrine of eschatology, which is the study of the prophetic Scriptures, provided the following insights.

> Daniel seems to have had no difficulty in interpreting the significance of the first three beasts. It was the fourth beast that caused him consternation, and he asked the angel (probably Gabriel; cf. 8:16; 9:21) to interpret the meaning of the beast and its 10 horns and the other horn that came up among the 10 and was so imposing. What is represented by the 10 horns and particularly the little horn is of great significance. For from this point on to the end of the prophecy, Daniel concerned himself with the revelation about the person and work of the

individual represented by this little horn. 7:21–22. Several facts about this little horn had already been revealed to Daniel (v. 8): (1) It came after the 10 horns (kings; cf. v. 24) were in existence and then was contemporaneous with them. (2) It uprooted 3 of the 10 horns (kings). (3) It was intelligent (it had the eyes of a man). (4) It was arrogant and boastful (cf. v. 11).[129]

The apostle John also discusses the arrival of the Antichrist in Revelation 13. John reveals the Antichrist comes on the global scene and gains the attention of the entire world. Exactly what the Antichrist does at first to gain the world's attention is unknown, outside of the fact that Revelation 6:1-2 appears to indicate that the Antichrist will use political prowess and not military might to gain the allegiance of the masses. The way he acquires a following and the literal worship of the populace, is by appearing to have been killed, and then miraculously he fully recovers, to the amazement and awe world's populace.

Then I stood on the sand of the sea. And I saw a beast *(Antichrist)* rising up out of the sea, having seven heads[130] and ten horns[131], and on his horns ten crowns, and on his heads a blasphemous name. Now the beast which I saw was like a leopard *(Greece: swiftness in conquering)*, his feet were like the feet of a bear *(Medo-Persia: Fierce Strength)*, and his mouth like the mouth of a lion *(Babylon: Consuming ferocious power)*. And I saw one of his heads as if it had been mortally wounded, and his deadly wound was healed. And all the world marveled and followed the beast. So they worshiped the dragon *(Satan)* who gave authority to the beast *(Antichrist)*; and they worshiped the beast, saying, "Who is like the beast? Who is able to make war with him?" (Rev. 13:1–4)

---

[129] J. Dwight Pentecost, "Daniel," in *The Bible Knowledge Commentary: An Exposition of the Scriptures*, ed. J. F. Walvoord and R. B. Zuck, vol. 1 (Wheaton, IL: Victor Books, 1985), 1353–1354.

[130] Seven heads refers to the following world empires in chronological order, including Egypt, Assyria, Babylon, Medo-Persia, Greece, Rome, and the yet future Revived Roman Empire.

[131] The ten horns and ten crowns refer to ten confederate nations that align with the Antichrist.

The Scriptures do not specify how the Antichrist receives the apparent deadly wound. While the Antichrist already had most people's attention, he needed something to occur that would arouse the devotion of the world's population and catapult him into a position of world dominance. Dwight Pentecost provides the following perspective.

> The final world ruler receives a wound which normally would be fatal but is miraculously healed by Satan. While the resurrection of a dead person seems to be beyond Satan's power, the healing of a wound would be possible for Satan, and this may be the explanation. The important point is that the final world ruler comes into power obviously supported by a supernatural and miraculous deliverance by Satan himself.[132]

The Detestable Character of the Antichrist

Daniel further reveals that this golden-tongued orator will speak with charismatic and dictatorial prowess, but he will also speak arrogantly against God and kill those who turn to faith in Jesus Christ, called *the saints*. "I was watching; and the same horn *(Antichrist)* was making war against the saints, and prevailing against them…He *(Antichrist)* shall speak pompous words against the Most High, shall persecute the saints of the Most High, and shall intend to change times and law. Then the saints shall be given into his hand for a time and times and half a time (3.5 years, 42 months, 1,260 days) (Dan. 7:21, 25).

The apostle Paul provides more insight into the Antichrist's detestable character. "Let no one deceive you by any means; for *that Day (the start of the seven-year Tribulation) will not come* unless the falling away comes first, and the man of sin *(Antichrist)* is revealed, the son of perdition, who opposes and exalts himself above all that is called God or that is worshiped, so that he sits as God in the temple of God, showing himself that he is God. Do you not remember that when I was still with you I told you these things" (2 Thess. 2:3-5)? Paul expands on an event called *the abomination of desolation*, when the Antichrist will break his peace treaty with the Jewish people and

---

[132] John F. Walvoord, "Revelation," in *The Bible Knowledge Commentary: An Exposition of the Scriptures*, ed. J. F. Walvoord and R. B. Zuck, vol. 2 (Wheaton, IL: Victor Books, 1985), 960.

desecrate the Jewish temple, also called the tabernacle in the book of Revelation.

> And he *(Antichrist)* was given a mouth speaking great things and blasphemies, and he was given authority to continue for forty-two months. Then he opened his mouth in blasphemy against God, to blaspheme His name, His tabernacle, and those who dwell in heaven. It was granted to him to make war with the saints and to overcome them. And authority was given him over every tribe, tongue, and nation. All who dwell on the earth will worship him, whose names have not been written in the Book of Life of the Lamb slain from the foundation of the world. (Revelation 13:5-8)

The Devil's Empowerment of the Antichrist

How does the Antichrist, a mere human being, gain massive power with apparent supernatural abilities? The answer lies in Revelation 12. God allows Satan access to Himself through the first half of the Tribulation. At the mid-point of the Tribulation, or after 3.5 years, God summons Michael, an elect angel, and his army of elect angels to cast Satan permanently out of heaven. Satan becomes infuriated with God because he knows that he only has 3.5 years to thwart God's program (Rev. 12:7-12).

At the start of Satan's 3.5 years on the earth, he will empower the Antichrist and propel him into position as the global dictator. The apostle John speaks to this exact fact.

> The dragon *(Satan)* gave him his power, his throne, and great authority. And *I saw* one of his heads as if it had been mortally wounded, and his deadly wound was healed. And all the world marveled and followed the beast. So they worshiped the dragon who gave authority to the beast; and they worshiped the beast, saying, "Who *is* like the beast? Who is able to make war with him?" (Rev. 13:2b-4)

The book of Revelation confirms the origin of the Antichrist's power a few verses later in Revelation 13:16. "The dragon *(Satan)* gave him *(Antichrist)* his power, his throne, and great authority." God reinforces this important piece of information to document the fact that Satan has done, is doing, and will do everything in his limited power to stop God's perfect prophetic program. Satan, although he knows the Scriptures (Matt. 4:6; Luke 4:9-12), still believes he can overcome God and become God (Isa. 14:14). Scripture makes it clear that Satan will lose in the end, and that everything God allows him to do will fulfill God's sovereign plan (Rev 20:10).

The Deadly Consequences of Rejecting the Antichrist

The prophetic Scriptures speak to the fact of the future satanic trinity, made up of Satan, Antichrist, and another person called the false prophet (Rev. 16:13; 19:20; 20:10). The apostle John refers to the false prophet as *another beast* in Revelation 13:11. The second beast, literally the person whom the Scriptures symbolically call the false prophet, will do everything he can to promote the Antichrist. This satanically led person will potentially incorporate the vast abilities of artificial intelligence and transhumanism to somehow know whether each person alive at that time follows the Antichrist's dictates in his one-world government, economy, and religion. The penalty for refusing to worship the Antichrist is the ultimate sanction: death.

> Then I saw another beast coming up out of the earth, and he had two horns like a lamb and spoke like a dragon. And he exercises all the authority of the first beast in his presence, and causes the earth and those who dwell in it to worship the first beast, whose deadly wound was healed. He performs great signs, so that he even makes fire come down from heaven on the earth in the sight of men. And he deceives those who dwell on the earth—by those signs which he was granted to do in the sight of the beast, telling those who dwell on the earth to make an image to the beast who was wounded by the sword and lived. He was granted power to give breath to the image of the beast, that the image of the beast should both speak and cause as many as would not worship the image of the beast to be killed. (Rev. 13:11–17)

Pause a moment to consider the dramatic outcome for those today who refuse to place their faith in the Lord Jesus Christ and receive His free gift of eternal life (John 3:16-17; Eph. 2:8-9). Should the Rapture of the Church-Age saints occur in this generation, all of those who did not place their faith in Christ will be left on this earth to face seven years of horrible tribulation. Should they survive the first three and a half years, they will face the devastating scenario of the satanic trinity. If they come to their senses, reject the mandates of the false prophet and the Antichrist, and place their faith in the Lord Jesus

Christ, they will in all probability face martyrdom unless they can somehow go underground and hide. The bad news is that they will probably face death. The good news is that upon dying, they will be absent from the body and immediately present with the Lord, based on their faith in Jesus Christ.

The major purpose of this book is to warn of the impending crisis towards which this world is rapidly heading and provide the only solution to escape the horrible outcomes of the global tyranny that the Scriptures guarantee will occur. The only hope for anyone, today or tomorrow, is to receive the gift of eternal life by placing one's faith in the One who paid the entire penalty for sin, Jesus Christ. Regardless of the trials and heartaches one faces today, the only way to find ultimate assurance for eternity is through Jesus Christ. "Jesus said to him, 'I am the way, the truth, and the life. No one comes to the Father except through Me'" (John 14:6). "For by grace you have been saved through faith, and that not of yourselves; it is the gift of God, not of works, lest anyone should boast. For we are His workmanship, created in Christ Jesus for good works, which God prepared beforehand that we should walk in them" (Eph. 2:8–10).

The Destruction of the Antichrist

God allows the Antichrist seven years on this earth. At the start of it, the Antichrist confirms a covenant, or peace treaty, with Israel. After 3.5 years, which is the midpoint of the Tribulation, the Antichrist breaks the treaty with Israel (Dan. 9:27). Also at that time, Satan loses his access to God; God has Satan and his demonic army cast to the earth. Satan is furious because he knows he only has 3.5 years to overcome God (Rev. 12:7-12). Therefore, Satan empowers the Antichrist and the false prophet to start the Great Tribulation (Luke 24:21), which for 3.5 years will bring unprecedented devastation upon the earth and its inhabitants (Dan. 9:27). The worst holocaust in history will occur during the Great Tribulation. Today, there are approximately 15 million Jews in the world. Zechariah 13:8-9 states that two-thirds of the Jewish people will die during the Tribulation period. Based on the current number of Jews living today, that means that 10 million Jews will die, which is 4 million more deaths than occurred during the holocaust.

God allows the satanic trinity incredible latitude during the Tribulation period to ultimately accomplish His will, in purging the world of those who reject Jesus Christ. The Scriptures reveal that the Lord Jesus Christ, the King of kings and Lord of lords, will return to the earth to finish the seven-year Tribulation and inaugurate his 1,000-year theocratic kingdom. When Jesus returns, He will remove the false prophet and the Antichrist from power, and cast them permanently into the lake of fire burning with brimstone, thus ending their reign of terror.

> And I saw the beast *(Antichrist)*, the kings of the earth, and their armies, gathered together to make war against Him who sat on the horse and against His army. Then the beast was captured, and with him the false prophet who worked signs in his presence, by which he deceived those who received the mark of the beast and those who worshiped his image. These two were cast alive into the lake of fire burning with brimstone. And the rest were killed with the sword which proceeded from the mouth of Him who sat on the horse. And all the birds were filled with their flesh. (Rev. 19:19-21)

God will also remove Satan from the earth during His 1,000-year millennial kingdom and bind him in the bottomless pit. "Then I saw an angel coming down from heaven, having the key to the bottomless pit and a great chain in his hand. He laid hold of the dragon, that serpent of old, who is the Devil and Satan, and bound him for a thousand years; and he cast him into the bottomless pit, and shut him up, and set a seal on him, so that he should deceive the nations no more till the thousand years were finished. But after these things he must be released for a little while" (Rev. 20:1-3). God will rule and reign on the earth in near Edenic conditions for the 1,000-year period. Almost shockingly, God releases Satan from the pit at the end of 1,000 years, allowing him to go throughout the earth and gather all the people who refused to trust in Jesus Christ, even though Jesus was physically present on the earth for the entire 1,000 years. Scripture reveals that as many people as the sand of the sea reject Jesus during His kingdom. The final place for Satan and all of those he gathers is the eternal lake of fire.

> Now when the thousand years have expired, Satan will be released from his prison and will go out to deceive the nations which are in the four corners of the earth, Gog and Magog, to gather them together to battle, whose number is as the sand of the sea. They went up on the breadth of the earth and

surrounded the camp of the saints and the beloved city *(Jerusalem)*. And fire came down from God out of heaven and devoured them. The devil, who deceived them, was cast into the lake of fire and brimstone where the beast and the false prophet are. And they will be tormented day and night forever and ever. (Revelation 20:7–10)

The great deceiver, Satan, along with the Antichrist and the false prophet, despite their impressive display of signs and wonders, including the potential use of advanced AI and transhumanism, will not succeed in their plot to destroy God and His people. The current question remains, who will allow themselves to be drawn into the satanic system and face eternal punishment; and who will turn to Jesus Christ in faith and receive the gift of eternal life, which He completely paid for through His death, burial, and resurrection (1 Cor. 15:1-4)?

CHAPTER SEVEN
GOD'S PROPHETIC TIMELINE

INTRODUCTION

God's unalterable prophetic timeline is key to understanding when AI and transhumanism could have their greatest negative global impact. There are two main theological positions regarding how God's prophetic calendar will materialize, specifically the dispensational and covenant interpretive models. The dispensational interpretive model adheres to the literal, historical, contextual, and grammatical hermeneutic[133] regarding the chronological sequence of events in Scripture. The covenant interpretive model incorporates spiritualizing and allegorizing the biblical texts, which fails to produce a solid, literal interpretation. Therefore, using the dispensational interpretive model, God's prophetic plan becomes very clear and precise. Simply stated, the dispensational interpretive model reveals how God works with specific people, in specific ways, at specific times.

The different dispensations can be seen throughout the Bible. For example, the Old Testament, which focuses on the Jewish people, is called the dispensation of law, referring to the Mosaic law. The New Testament focuses on the life and work of Jesus Christ in the gospels, and then on the Church Age, which is the present dispensation. The inspired New Testament writers (2 Tim. 3:16) tell about the Jews and Gentiles who did not accept Jesus Christ as their Savior, and the Church-Age believers in Jesus Christ (Jews and Gentiles who did convert to Christianity). God reveals His prophetic timeline for the Jewish people in Daniel 9:24-27 and expands on those prophecies in many other passages. God reveals the timeline for the Church-Age saints in multiple passages throughout the New Testament.

The Scriptures reveal God's prophetic calendar of events in chronological order as follows: the next major event is the Rapture of the Church-Age believers in Jesus Christ (1 Thess. 4:13-18; 1 Cor. 15:50-54), which is followed by the seven-year Tribulation period (Dan. 9:26; Matthew 24:4-28; Rev. 6-18), the second advent (the

---

[133] Bernard Ramm, *Protestant Biblical Interpretation* (Grand Rapids: Baker Book House, 1970), 119, 136, 138.

return of Jesus Christ to earth to set up his one-thousand-year Millennial Kingdom (Rev. 20:1-7)), the destruction of the current heavens and earth (2 Pet. 3:7), and the inauguration of eternity future, where every person ever born will spend eternity either with the Lord or in the lake of fire (Eph. 2:2-9; Rev. 21:8). There are many other events that Scripture reveals will take place, but this book, which focuses on AI, transhumanism, and the de-evolution of democracy, is more directly concerned with the coming seven-year Tribulation period.

During the Tribulation period, Satan, Antichrist, and the false prophet (Rev. 16:13), the satanic false trinity, will in all probability use advanced technology in the most devastating ways to control the world and mandate the one-world government, economy, and religion (Rev. 13). Though this may seem inconceivable, consider the fact that there are approximately 1,000 prophecies in the Bible. God has already fulfilled 500 of those prophecies exactly as written, which means God has yet to fulfill precisely the remaining 500 prophecies.[134] The documentation on what God has brought to exact fulfillment is astounding, and yes, miraculous. God's record is perfect and without error. Therefore, be assured that every prophecy discussed in this section will come to exact fulfillment.

This chapter examines what God created in perfect splendor, including the angelic realm, this earth and all that it contains (Gen. 1:32), and how Satan subsequently attacked God's perfect theocratic kingdom, causing humankind to fall from perfection, to individuals in need of a Savior, whom God would subsequently identify as Jesus Christ (Gen. 3:1-24; John 3:16). The prophetic scenario includes Satan's continual attack during the seven-year Tribulation, where the evil satanic trinity will do everything within their limited power to thwart God's prophetic plan. This, once again, is where Satan, Antichrist, and the false prophet will incorporate every tool available to them, including what appears to be AI and transhumanism, to form and control the one-world system.

The Satanic Kingdom

The Scriptures are replete with Satan's attempts to rule his own kingdom and to attack God with the goal of stopping His ultimate plan of redeeming lost sinners and ultimately setting up His eternal kingdom (Gen. 3; Ex. 1:15-18; Est. 3-

---

[134] John Walvoord, *Every Prophecy of the Bible,* (David C. Cook, Colorado Springs, CO.: 2011), 7.

9; Isa. 14:12-15; Matt. 2:17-18; Lk. 4:28-30). Despite Satan's guaranteed defeat by God, he has, is and will continue to fight against God and His people until he faces his eternal destiny in the lake of fire (Rev. 20:10).

God created the angelic world on the first day of creation, which included the perfectly created angel who would subsequently rebel against God and become His eternal enemy (Isa. 14:12-14; Ez. 28:13-18). Satan convinced one third of the perfectly created angels to rebel against God, thus forming the horde of demonic angels (Rev. 12:4). Satan's rebellion against God occurred shortly after his creation. Genesis chapters one and two record the six days of creation, culminating in the creation of Adam and Eve, the first two human beings. Genesis chapter three records Satan's attack against the couple, and their subsequent rebellion against the commandment of God not to eat the forbidden fruit. Satan experienced his first success in establishing his reign of terror against the true God (Gen. 3:1-6).

In Genesis chapter six, the Scriptures record what some theologians conclude was the demonic world having sexual relations with human females, resulting in the birth of a forbidden class of people (Gen. 6:1-5). Other interpreters view the "sons of god" who had relations with the daughters of men as evil descendants from the line of Seth.[135] Concluding that the "sons of god" refers to the demonic realm accentuates the act of Satan and his demonic followers to establish their own peculiar race of people to build his kingdom. The fact that nearly all humanity rejected their Creator, resulted in God's wrath and the devastating worldwide Flood, which destroyed all living beings except for Noah, his immediate family members, and the animals who entered Noah's ark (Gen. 6:1-8:19).

Satan's efforts to establish his evil kingdom rose to the forefront again in Genesis chapter ten when the people, under the leadership of Nimrod, the great grandson of Adam, rebelled against the commandment of God to disperse across the earth (Gen. 9:1). Instead, Nimrod established the great city of Babylon, built the tower of Babel, and attempted to establish a false religion. God subsequently destroyed the tower, instituted different languages, and scattered the people throughout the known world (Gen. 11:1-

---

[135] John H. Sailhamer, "Genesis," ed. Frank E. Gaebelein, in *The Expositor's Bible Commentary* (Grand Rapids: Zondervan, 1990), 76.

9).[136]

Scripture clearly states that Satan is the "god of this world." However, the satanic kingdom shall never overcome the sovereign will of God (2 Cor. 4:3-4; Jn. 12:31). The Gentile world powers that have existed since the Babylonian empire, establishing the "times of the Gentiles" (Lk. 21:24) defined as, anytime in history when the Gentiles have control over the Jewish people and the city of Jerusalem, will end when the Lord Jesus Christ returns to the earth at the end of the Tribulation period. Jesus Christ subsequently conquers the satanic Gentile world power and establishes His Millennial Kingdom (Matt 25:36-41; Rev. 19:11-20:7).

Two Godly Kingdoms

Alva McClain strongly contends that the Bible clearly reveals two aspects, or phases, of God's sovereign rule in His kingdom, which he refers to as the *Universal Kingdom* and the *Mediatorial Kingdom*. The Universal Kingdom regards God's rule over the universe from eternity past through eternity future. The Mediatorial Kingdom specifically concerns God's dealings with humanity on the earth, specifically during the eschatological Millennial Kingdom.[137]

The Universal Kingdom

McClain takes a strong position regarding the existence of the Universal Kingdom of God, which he states has existed throughout history without interruption. McClain cites Psalm 145:13, "Thy kingdom is an everlasting kingdom" as his proof text. Additionally, Scripture reveals, "The Lord sat enthroned at the Flood, And the Lord sits as King forever" (Ps. 29:10), and God is "the true God, he is the living God, and an everlasting king" (Jer. 10:2-5, 10).138 McClain argues the reality of the Universal Kingdom by stating, "The historical Kingdom of God in Israel may be interrupted; the nation may abide for many days without a Mediatorial king; but there is nevertheless

---

[136] Jimmy DeYoung, *Isaiah the Beloved Prophet*, Audio Series (Chattanooga: Prophecy Today, 2011). CD 3, Track 2.
[137] Alva J. McClain, *The Greatness of the Kingdom* (Winona Lake, BMH Books, 1974) 21.
[138] Ibid.

a Kingdom of God which continues without any hiatus or diminution."[139]

The scope of the Universal Kingdom includes all that exists in time and space. It includes the totality of the creation, including the heavens, the earth, the grave, hell, angels, and all created beings, including humanity. Scripture concludes that nothing exists outside of the Universal Kingdom of God (Ps. 103:19-22; Amos 9:2). The Psalmist reiterates this truth: "Where can I go from Your Spirit? Or where can I flee from Your presence? If I ascend into heaven, You are there; If I make my bed in hell, behold, You are there. If I take the wings of the morning, And dwell in the uttermost parts of the sea, Even there Your hand shall lead me, And Your right hand shall hold me" (Ps. 139:7-10).

God generally controls His Universal Kingdom via providential means, which McClain defines as secondary causes. For example, in the Exodus account of the parting of the Red Sea, God used a "strong east wind" to part the waters. God could have simply commanded the waters to part, which would be considered a primary movement by God. However, He chose to use the primary command to order the east wind to part the Red Sea by His providential, or secondary intervention (Ex. 14:21). God providentially intervenes in the affairs of humanity to bring about His perfect will. McClain further states, "Christians must never forget the unseen 'finger of God' whose touch always brings the final decision in the affairs of the universe. This is the providential factor."[140]

The Universal Kingdom of God is distinct from the Mediatorial Kingdom, specifically, the eschatological, physical, millennial reign of Jesus Christ the Messiah on earth. McClain makes the following observation:

> The great purpose of the Mediatorial Kingdom appears: On the basis of Mediatorial redemption it must 'come' to put down at last all rebellion with its train of evil results, thus finally bringing the Kingdom and will of God on earth as it is in heaven. When this purpose has been fully accomplished, the Mediatorial phase of the Kingdom will disappear as a

---

[139] Ibid.
[140] Ibid.

separate entity, being merged with the Universal Kingdom of God.[141]

Renald Showers adds that the Theocratic Kingdom of God "is restricted to God's rule over the earth; it does not involve His rule over the entire universe."[142] Great theological and interpretive caution must be exercised when attempting to spiritualize or allegorize any Scriptural text referring to the Millennial Kingdom, and improperly applying the passages to the current Church Age. Such poor hermeneutics leads to the errors of covenant, supersessionist, and replacement theology, which claim that God will not fulfill the unconditional covenant promises He made to Israel. Such is not the case; God will fulfill His word!

The Theocratic Kingdom

The magnificent Millennial Kingdom of the Lord Jesus Christ constitutes an eschatological one-thousand-year event. This section examines prophesies and events that must occur prior to the inauguration of the Kingdom. In addition, we will examine the summary facts regarding the Theocratic Ruler and the significant changes that will occur during the Kingdom.

Prophecies of the Messianic Kingdom

Numerous prophetic scriptural passages describe the arrival of the future eschatological Millennial Kingdom. God gave the prophet Daniel a specific prophetic outline of the empires that would exist from the time Daniel wrote the prophecy, approximately 536 B.C., through the inauguration of the Millennial Kingdom. Daniel wrote the prophecy from Babylon, where the Jewish people were held captive for seventy years. God outlined several changes in empires that would occur before the Kingdom. The historical record shows that four of the empires already have risen and fallen from power, including Babylon, Medo-Persia, Greece, and Rome (Dan.

---

[141] Ibid. Alva J. McClain, *The Greatness of the Kingdom* (Winona Lake, BMH Books, 1974) 21.
[142] Renald E. Showers, *There Really is a Difference! A Comparison of Covenant and Dispensational Theology* (Bellmawr: The Friends of Israel Gospel Ministry, Inc., 1990), 161.

2:36-41).[143] After the Rapture of the Church, the revived Roman Empire comes to power, ruled by the Antichrist, which will last seven years. Then the Lord Jesus Christ returns to the earth and inaugurates His Millennial Kingdom.

> As you saw iron mixed with ceramic clay, they will mingle with the seed of men; but they will not adhere to one another, just as iron does not mix with clay. And in the days of these kings the God of heaven will set up a kingdom which shall never be destroyed; and the kingdom shall not be left to other people; it shall break in pieces and consume all these kingdoms, and it shall stand forever. Inasmuch as you saw that the stone was cut out of the mountain without hands, and that it broke in pieces the iron, the bronze, the clay, the silver, and the gold—the great God has made known to the king what will come to pass after this. The dream is certain, and its interpretation is sure. (Daniel 2:44-45)

Stephen Miller rightly concludes that the feet and the toes constitute the end times phase of the revived Roman Empire. Therefore, "the establishment of Christ's rule at his second advent during the time of these kings is the meaning of the rock striking the statue upon its feet and toes."[144]

Later in the book of Daniel, God repeated His promise of the Millennial Kingdom, "And the kingdom and dominion, and the greatness of the kingdom under the whole heaven, shall be given to the people of the saints of the most High, whose kingdom *is* an everlasting kingdom, and all dominions shall serve and obey him" (Dan. 7:27). The "times of the Gentiles" will come to an end after the seven-year Tribulation period when the Lord Jesus Christ returns to inaugurate His Millennial Kingdom.[145]

The most detailed prophesy concerning the exact span of time for the Messianic Theocratic Kingdom resides in the book of Revelation. John, the author of the book of Revelation under the inspiration of God, specifically states six times that the Kingdom remains for one thousand years, or a millennium (Rev. 20:1-7). No reason exists to discount a literal interpretation of the one-thousand-

---

[143] John F. Walvoord, *Daniel*, ed. Charles H. Dyer and Philip E. Rawley (Chicago: Moody Publishers, 2012), 80-83.
[144] DeYoung, *Sound the Trumpets*, 110-111.
[145] Walvoord, *The Millennial Kingdom*, 257.

year physical reign of Jesus Christ on earth. The covenant, replacement, and supersessionist theologians allegorize and spiritualize this passage to the point of denying the literal fulfillment of the Millennial Kingdom, resulting in their embracing the highly suspect amillennial position.[146]

The Jewish people have been looking for the Messiah to come and set up His earthly kingdom for thousands of years. While they understand the reality of the future Theocratic Kingdom of the Messiah, most Jewish people have failed to understand the necessity of the Lord Jesus Christ's first advent to sacrifice Himself to pay for the sins of humanity. One day in the eschatological future, the remnant of the Jewish people will turn to the Lord Jesus Christ and embrace Him as their Messiah and King (Rom. 9:27; 11:26).

Presentation of the Messianic Kingdom by Jesus

The Lord Jesus Christ, during His earthly ministry, made a legitimate offer of His Kingdom specifically to the Jewish people and Gentile proselytes. Matthew chapters 5 through 7 contain what is often called the Sermon on the Mount. Dr. Jimmy DeYoung writes that the Sermon on the Mount represented the legitimate offer of the Kingdom.[147] That sermon described the pattern of behavior that the Lord expected from His followers during His reign on earth. When Jesus Christ preached that sermon, three groups of people were present: the Sadducees and the Pharisees, a massive group of followers (as attested to by the feeding of the 5,000 and 4,000 men, plus woman and children) (Matt. 14:21; 15:38), and the Lord's own disciples. All those people heard the Lord Jesus Christ legitimately offer them the Kingdom of God; unfortunately, most of them would subsequently reject that offer.[148]

The Lord Jesus Christ clearly stated that the "gospel of the Kingdom" was preached during His earthly ministry (Matt. 4:23; 9:35; 24:14; Mk. 1:14). This stands in contrast to the "gospel of the grace of God," which has been preached since the start of the Church Age (Acts 20:24).[149] Following the Rapture of the Church-Age saints, the "gospel of the Kingdom" shall once again be preached during the

---

[146] Showers, 167.
[147] Jimmy DeYoung, *Kingdom Come* (Chattanooga, Shofar Communications, 2015) Video.
[148] Ibid.
[149] Ibid.

seven-year Tribulation period, because the Lord stated in the Olivet Discourse, "And this gospel of the kingdom shall be preached in all the world for a witness unto all nations; and then shall the end come" (Matt. 24:14). This passage highlights the importance of using proper hermeneutics when interpreting Scripture. The false teaching exists that the gospel must reach all people before the Rapture occurs. Though reaching all people with the gospel of Jesus Christ constitutes an appropriate goal (2 Cor. 5:18-21), there is no Church-Age mandate that all the world hear the gospel before the Rapture occurs.

In the Sermon on the Mount, the Lord Jesus Christ taught His disciples a prayer that carried great eschatological significance (Matt. 6:9-13). The prayer, commonly known as The Lord's Prayer, is recited in many churches, specifically in certain denominational churches. Those reciting the prayer in services or in their daily prayer time, in all probability, fail to understand its exact meaning. However, when applying dispensational hermeneutics in interpreting the prayer, and applying it to the current Church Age, the results are suspect. The specific part of the prayer, with a stated nexus to the future eschatological kingdom, contains the instruction to pray, "Your kingdom come. Your will be done on earth, as *it is* in heaven" (Matt. 6:10). Jesus was preparing His disciples for the next major events on God's Jewish prophetic calendar. There was an expectation that, following the Lord's death, burial, resurrection, and ascension, the prophesied seventieth week of Daniel's prophecy would be fulfilled; that is, the seven-year Tribulation period that God designed to prepare the world for the return of the Lord Jesus Christ to inaugurate His Millennial Kingdom (Dan. 9:27; Rev. 19:11-16; Rev. 20:1-7).

The Church Age was an unknown concept to the disciples, as the Scriptures state that the Church Age was kept a mystery (not revealed) until after the ascension of Jesus Christ (Eph. 3:1-7; Col. 1:24-29). Christians anticipate the imminent Rapture of the Church, not the Millennial Kingdom.[150] Once the Rapture of the Church Age saints occurs, it makes perfect theological sense for those remaining on the earth during the seven-year Tribulation to pray the Lord's prayer. When believers face catastrophic conditions during the Tribulation, they shall indeed look forward to the second coming of Jesus Christ to crush His enemies and inaugurate His Kingdom.

---

[150] Ibid.

Therefore, as Jesus currently resides in heaven at His Father's right hand (Heb. 1:3; 8:1; 10:12; 12:2), He shall one day fulfill His rightful place as the theocratic ruler of the Kingdom on earth.[151]

Postponement of the Messianic Kingdom

The Lord Jesus preached the gospel of the Kingdom, making a legitimate offer to His listeners to make Him their King and to inaugurate His kingdom on earth. However, the overwhelming majority of people rejected the offer. Matthew recorded the words of Jesus as He reviewed His rejection in three major cities where He had preached and ministered: Chorazin, Bethsaida, and Capernaum.

> Then He began to rebuke the cities in which most of His mighty works had been done, because they did not repent: "Woe to you, Chorazin! Woe to you, Bethsaida! For if the mighty works which were done in you had been done in Tyre and Sidon, they would have repented long ago in sackcloth and ashes. But I say to you, it will be more tolerable for Tyre and Sidon in the day of judgment than for you. And you, Capernaum, who are exalted to heaven, will be brought down to Hades; for if the mighty works which were done in you had been done in Sodom, it would have remained until this day. But I say to you that it shall be more tolerable for the land of Sodom in the day of judgment than for you." (Matthew 11:20-24)

The Jewish people rejected the Messiah and therefore rejected the offer of His kingdom. However, the Theocratic Kingdom did not suffer a fatal blow. God postponed the inauguration of the Messianic Kingdom as revealed in the prophetic Scriptures. Matthew then recorded the words of the rejected Messiah when the Jews asked Him to provide yet another sign to authenticate that He was truly the Messiah. Jesus responded by citing the historical fact, which the Jews knew, regarding Jonah's confinement in the great fish for three days and three nights. Jesus stated that He also would be three days and three nights in the heart of the earth (Matt. 12:39-41). Jesus officially postponed the inauguration of His Kingdom, and instead would fulfill His mission of going to the cross to pay for the sins of humanity (Lk. 19:10; Jn. 3:16-17; Rom. 5:8).

---

[151] Ibid.

Stanley Toussaint rightly contends that the Jewish people as a whole rejected Jesus Christ as their King during His so-called triumphal entry into Jerusalem during His passion week. The crowds welcomed Jesus as He rode into Jerusalem on the humble donkey. The people threw down their garments and tree branches to show respect for Him. However, despite their apparent acceptance, Matthew records the inconsistent response of the people who were seemingly welcoming their King: When they were asked, "Who is this?" the response was, "This is the prophet, Jesus from Nazareth in Galilee" (Matt. 21:10-21:11). The people did not recognize Jesus as the King, but simply as a prophet.[152] Within a few days, the people would demand and secure His crucifixion.

Precursors of the Messianic Kingdom

Scripture clearly designates multiple events that must take place before the inauguration of the Millennial Kingdom of Jesus Christ. The two overarching periods that must be fulfilled before the commencement of the Millennial, Theocratic Kingdom are the Church Age and the seven-year Tribulation. This section examines those two periods, which serve as the precursors to the Messianic Kingdom.

The Mystery Church Revealed

God specifically chose to keep the Church Age a mystery during the Old Testament period (Eph. 3:1-7; Col. 1:24-29). A careful exegesis of Daniel's 70-week prophecy reveals that the current Church Age was not revealed in God's prophetic timetable (Dan 9:24-27).

The 70-week prophecy covers 70 heptads, or groupings of 7, which biblical scholars rightly determine to be 70 groupings of 7 years, or 490 years. Performing the math, 69 of the 70 years occurred in the past, which equates to 483 years. Daniel 9:26 records the conclusion of the 69th week. According to Sir Robert Anderson, the 69th week concluded on the very day that Jesus entered Jerusalem in His "triumphal entry."[153] Furthermore, the first 69 weeks, or 483

---

[152] Stanley D. Toussaint, *Behold the King, A Study of Matthew* (Portland, Multnomah, 1980), 241.

[153] Sir Robert Anderson, *The Coming Prince* (Grand Rapids, Kregel Publishing, 1975), 127-128.

years, continued without a single break or gap. However, dispensational scholars strongly contend that a gap of time exists between the 69th and 70th weeks of Daniel's prophecy, which has existed for over 1,985 years. This distinctly dispensational position argues for the current literal Church Age, which God chose to keep a mystery until after the ascension of Jesus Christ (Eph. 3:1-7; Col. 1:24-29). The current Church Age occurs between the 69th and 70th weeks of Daniel's prophecy, or literally between Daniel 9:26 and 27.[154] Daniel 9:27 discusses the confirmation of a covenant that the eschatological Antichrist makes with the Jewish people. That confirmation marks the beginning of the seven-year Tribulation period.[155]

Therefore, the Church Age has no link to the Old Testament prophetic calendar. God inserted the mystery Church Age into His sovereignly designed plan of the ages. The Church cannot constitute the Kingdom Age, when interpreting Scripture with a proper literal hermeneutic. Therefore, Alva McClain rightly states, "Since the Church is present in history, it cannot be the Kingdom. Neither can the Church bring in the Kingdom or advance it."[156]

The Mystery Church Raptured

The Church Age must come to an end before God's prophetic calendar, as outlined in Daniel 9:24-27, is restarted. Scripture indicates that the Rapture, of the Church-Age saints marks the end of the Church Age.

> But I do not want you to be ignorant, brethren, concerning those who have fallen asleep, lest you sorrow as others who have no hope. For if we believe that Jesus died and rose again, even so God will bring with Him those who sleep in Jesus. For this we say to you by the word of the Lord, that we who are alive and remain until the coming of the Lord will by no means precede those who are asleep. For the Lord Himself will descend from heaven with a shout, with the voice of an archangel, and with the trumpet of God. And the dead in Christ will rise first. Then we who are alive and remain shall

---

[154] Walvoord, *Daniel*, 284.
[155] Paul N. Benware, *Understanding End Times Prophecy* (Chicago: Moody Publishers, 2006), 306.
[156] McClain, 14.

be caught up together with them in the clouds to meet the Lord in the air. And thus we shall always be with the Lord. Therefore comfort one another with these words. (1 Thess. 4:13-18).

The Apostle Paul provided a companion passage in 1 Corinthians that elaborates on the Rapture of the Church-Age saints. Now this I say, brethren, that flesh and blood cannot inherit the kingdom of God; nor does corruption inherit incorruption. Behold, I tell you a mystery: We shall not all sleep, but we shall all be changed—in a moment, in the twinkling of an eye, at the last trumpet. For the trumpet will sound, and the dead will be raised incorruptible, and we shall be changed. For this corruptible must put on incorruption, and this mortal must put on immortality. So when this corruptible has put on incorruption, and this mortal has put on immortality, then shall be brought to pass the saying that is written: "Death is swallowed up in victory." (1 Cor. 15:50-53).

Once the Rapture of the Church-Age saints occurs, God's prophetic timeline resumes, and Daniel 9:27 becomes the next major event before the second coming of Jesus Christ (Rev. 19:11-16) to earth and the inauguration of the literal one-thousand-year Messianic Kingdom (Rev. 20:1-7).[157]

The Mandatory Seven-Year Tribulation Period

The Rapture of the Church-Age saints, which was not revealed to Old Testament prophets, marks the completion of the Church Age. Then, as the dispensational model of biblical interpretation strongly concludes, the prophetic timeline of Daniel 9:24-27 resumes. The Church Age began after the end of the 69th week of Daniel's prophecy, which corresponds to the triumphal entry of Jesus Christ into Jerusalem, during His passion week (Dan. 9:26).[158] A nearly 2,000-year gap exists to date between Daniel 9:26 and 9:27, and that gap will continue until the Rapture occurs (1 Thess. 4:13-

---

[157] Jimmy DeYoung, *Sound the Trumpets* (Chattanooga: Shofar Communications, 2000), 12-13.
[158] Anderson, 127-128.

18). Shortly after the Rapture, the Antichrist shall confirm a covenant with the Jewish people, at which time God's prophetic timeline resumes and the eschatological seven-year Tribulation period begins (Dan. 9:27). Scripture is replete with references to this seven-year period of judgment, which is a definite precursor to the coming of the King, Jesus Christ. The Tribulation plays a major part in purging the world of those who oppose the Lord Jesus Christ (Matt. 24-25; Rev. 6-19). The satanic trinity will incorporate every means possible, including AI and potentially transhumanism, to deceive and control the world, as they implement the one-world government, economy, and religion (Rev. 13). The Lord Jesus returns to earth directly after the Tribulation period (Matt. 24:29).[159]

Among the many eschatological events that take place during the Tribulation is the alignment of the nations against Israel. Ezekiel 38-39 and Daniel 11 describe the nations that will rise up to destroy Israel. Currently, the religion of the nations described in these passages is of the Muslim or Islamic faith. The nations that rise up against Israel include the Old Testament names of Magog (modern-day Russia); Meshech, Tubal, Gomer, and Togarmah (modern-day Turkey); Persia (modern-day Afghanistan), Pakistan and Iran; Cush, which includes Somalia, Sudan and Ethiopia, and Put (modern-day Libya). Ezekiel prophesied that God would destroy the stated nations during the first half of the Tribulation period (Ez. 38:18-22).[160]

Jesus described many of the eschatological events that would take place during the Tribulation, all precursors to the Millennial Kingdom. Jesus stated that there would be great religious deception; that individuals would arise claiming they are the Messiah (Matt. 24:4-5, 11, 23-27); and that there would be wars and rumors of wars, emphasizing the violence of the times (Matt. 24:6-7). The worldwide situation will be chaotic with famines, pestilences, and earthquakes (Matt. 24:7). Believers in the Lord shall suffer extreme persecution and martyrdom (Matt. 24:9-10). At the mid-point of the Tribulation, the Antichrist shall desecrate the third Jewish Temple and set himself up as God, resulting in the most devastating anti-God satanic persecution since Creation (Matt. 24:15, 21-22). The Lord illustrated the inattentive mindset of the people to their spirituality during the

---

[159] DeYoung, *Kingdom Come*, Video.
[160] DeYoung, *Sound the Trumpets*, 68-69.

Tribulation. He compared it to the spiritual condition of the people who lived prior to the catastrophic worldwide Flood in the days of Noah. The people lived for themselves in earthly fleshly pleasures and ignored their Creator. They had no idea that they would soon be destroyed by the Flood. Jesus clearly stated that the same exact conditions shall exist during the Great Tribulation, and they shall be severely judged by the Messiah when He returns to inaugurate His Kingdom (Matt. 24:36-39). The one very positive outcome during the Tribulation is that the gospel of the kingdom is preached to every person on earth (Matt. 24:14). However, as Jesus stated, those trusting in the Lord shall suffer persecution and face martyrdom.

In the Olivet Discourse, Jesus described the final events before His literal second coming. "Immediately after the tribulation of those days the sun will be darkened, and the moon will not give its light; the stars will fall from heaven, and the powers of the heavens will be shaken. Then the sign of the Son of Man will appear in heaven" (Matt. 24:29-30a).

Jesus emphasized that His prophecy would come to pass exactly as stated. "Heaven and earth shall pass away, but my words shall not pass away (Matt. 24:35). Therefore, Jesus Himself, in the Olivet Discourse, absolutely and unequivocally guaranteed He shall return to earth again to establish His Millennial Kingdom.

Scripture provides numerous names and descriptors for the seven-year Tribulation period. The "Day of the Lord" is defined by Dr. DeYoung as any time in history when God intercedes in the affairs of man, personally on the earth, and refers to three specific time periods, including the entire Tribulation period, the specific one day when the Lord Jesus returns to earth, and the Millennial Kingdom (Isa. 2:12; 13:6-9; Joel 1:1:15; 2:1, 11, 31; 3:14; Zeph. 1:7, 14; Zech. 14:1). The Tribulation is also called "trouble" (Deut. 4:30), "time of Jacob's trouble" (Jer. 30:7), "birth pangs" (Isa. 21:3; 26:17-18; Jer. 4:31; Mic. 4:10), "the day of calamity" (Deut. 32:35; Ob. 12-14), "indignation" (Isa. 26:20; Dan. 11:36), "overflowing scourge" (Isa. 28:15-18), "day of vengeance" (Isa. 34:8; 35:4; 61:2; 63:4), "day of wrath" (Zeph. 1:15), "day of the Lord's wrath" (Zeph. 1:18), "day of distress" (Zeph. 1:15), "day of destruction" (Zeph. 1:15), "day of darkness and gloom" (Joel 2:2; Amos 5:18, 20; Zeph. 1:15), "day of trumpet and alarm" (Zeph. 1:16), "day of the Lord's anger" (Zeph. 2:2-3), destruction, ruin from the Almighty" (Joel 1:15), and "the fire of His jealousy" (Zeph. 1:18).[161] The names associated with the Tribulation describe the catastrophic events and conditions that occur during the time of purging the earth in preparation for the coming of the Messiah at His second advent.

One of the key events during the Tribulation is the construction of the third Jewish temple in Jerusalem. The Temple Mount in the old city of Jerusalem is the structure where the first two Jewish temples resided (the first temple in 960 B.C.–586 B.C., the second temple in 515 B.C.–A.D. 70), and which currently is the platform for the Muslim al-Aqsa Mosque and the Dome of the Rock shrine. Scripture reveals that an eschatological, Tribulation temple shall exist (Dan. 9:27; Matt. 24:15; 2 Thess. 2:4; Rev. 11:1). Shortly after the Rapture of the Church-Age saints, the Antichrist shall confirm a covenant with the people of Israel, which according to Daniel 9:27 results in the construction of the third, or Tribulation temple. The new temple provides the venue for the Jewish people to reinstate the sacrificial offerings. However, the Antichrist stops the temple sacrifices in the middle of the Tribulation period or after three and a half years, performs the anti-God abomination of desolation in the temple, and forbids the Jewish people from worshipping God henceforth (Dan. 9:17; 2 Thess. 2:4; Matt. 24:15).[162]

Revelation documents that a satanic false religious system shall exist during the first three and a half years of the Tribulation (Rev. 17). At the mid-point of the Tribulation period, God casts Satan out of heaven to earth (Rev.12:12). Satan subsequently empowers the Antichrist and the False Prophet, resulting in the destruction of the false religious system. The Antichrist then inaugurates his own satanically powered one-world religion, requiring mandatory adherence (Rev. 12:9-12; 13; 17:17).[163]

God warned the Jewish people, who are alive during the Tribulation period, to flee their land when the Antichrist commits the horrific sacrilege in the Temple, referred to as the Abomination of Desolation (Matt. 24:15-16). God promised to protect the remnant of the Jewish people in a secured area, which according to Scripture

---

[161] J. Randall Price, "Old Testament References to the Tribulation," in *Dictionary of Premillennial Theology*, ed. Mal Couch (Grand rapids: Kregel Publishing, 1996) 412-413.

[162] J. Randall Price, "The Future Temple," in *Dictionary of Premillennial Theology*, ed. Mal Couch (Grand Rapids: Kregel Publishing, 1996), 404-405.

[163] DeYoung, *Sound the Trumpets*, 110-111.

is Bozrah or Petra in Jordan (Isa. 63:1; Mic. 2:12). The horrific events of the Tribulation indicate to those alive at the time that the Messiah will shortly return to earth. Jesus Himself provided numerous parables, specific to the Jewish people living during the Tribulation, exhorting them to live for the Lord, and to prepare and watch for His physical, literal appearance when He judges the unrighteous and establishes His Millennial Kingdom (Matt. 13).[164]

Two other major prerequisites occur before the second coming of Jesus Christ to establish His Millennial Kingdom. Revelation 18 reveals that literal Babylon becomes a worldwide economic center during the Tribulation. The business people of the world are enamored with the great goods and wealth of the city. However, as the end of the Tribulation draws near, John prophesied that in Babylon, 'Alas, alas, that great city, in which all who had ships on the sea became rich by her wealth! For in one hour she is made desolate' (Rev. 18:19).

The final major event preceding the second advent of Christ is the campaign of Armageddon (Rev 16:16; 19:15-18). Zechariah prophesied that "all nations" shall gather together in Israel, specifically the Valley of Megiddo, to fight against the Jewish people and the Lord Himself. This event is the last major prerequisite for the return of the Lord Jesus. Jesus returns to earth at the Mount of Olives and destroys the soldiers of the nations by His word at the final battle of Armageddon (Zech. 14; Rev. 19:15, 21). The satanic trinity comes to an abrupt end, as the Antichrist and the False Prophet are sent to the lake of fire, and Satan is bound, preventing him from securing any access to the earth during the Millennial Kingdom (Rev. 19:19-20).[165]

Positive Guarantee of the Messianic Kingdom

The Scriptures dogmatically state that the eschatological, Messianic, Millennial Kingdom shall come to fulfillment. There are multiple promises that God made to the Jewish people guaranteeing the future inauguration of the Kingdom. Four of those promises are

---

[164] Roy E. Beacham, "The Parables of the Kingdom" in *Dictionary of Premillennial Theology*, ed. Mal Couch (Grand Rapids: Kregel Publishing, 1996), 233-234.
[165] Edward Hindson, "Battle of Armageddon," In *Dictionary of Premillennial Theology*. Editor Mal Couch. Grand Rapids: Kregel Publications, 1996. 56-57.

specific to four covenants God made between Himself and the Jewish people. The covenants summarized in this section, consist of the Abrahamic, Land, Davidic, and New Covenants.

Abrahamic Covenant

God presented the Abrahamic Covenant in Genesis 12:1-3. God promised Abraham a specific piece of land (known as Israel), a great nation from his descendants, blessings for his people, blessings on those who bless Abraham's descendants, and curses upon those who curse his people, resulting in all the people of the earth receiving blessings through Abraham, which comes to fulfillment in the Millennial Kingdom. The covenant regards an eschatological fulfillment, as the complete fulfillment has yet to occur. God shall fulfill the covenant, as God only speaks truth (Heb. 6:18).[166]

The covenant promise that God made with Abraham (Gen 12:2-3, 7; 13:15; 17:8) was passed down through his descendants. God confirmed the Abrahamic covenant with Isaac (Gen. 26:3) and Jacob (Gen. 28:13; 35:12) and their descendants. God subsequently changed Jacob's name to Israel, from which his sons would form the twelve tribes of Israel (Gen 35:10). The Abrahamic covenant shall fully come to fruition when Jesus Christ establishes His Millennial Kingdom.[167]

Davidic Covenant

The covenant God made with King David is regarded as a "grant" covenant, in contrast to the Mosaic covenant which is regarded as a "suzerain-vassal" treaty, and looks forward to the establishment of the ultimate reign of God on earth.[168] The Davidic covenant contains several eschatological promises (2 Sam 7:8-16). When introducing the Davidic covenant, God stated that He made the covenant "for my people Israel" who would "dwell in a place of their own," Israel (2 Sam. 7:10). The covenant promises that one from David's line would sit "in the house," referring to the Millennial Temple (2 Sam. 7:12-14, 16; Ez. 40-46). The covenant mandates that the Messiah must come from the line of David to accomplish the

---

[166] Arnold G. Fruchtenbaum, *The Footsteps of the Messiah* (San Antonio: Ariel Ministries, 2004), 420.
[167] Ibid., 421-424.
[168] Michael A. Grisanti, "The Davidic Covenant," *TMSJ* (Fall 1999), 233.

prophesy of the Messiah's line, to take His place as the King of kings in the Millennial Kingdom, and to take His throne that shall last forever. Scripture confirms that Jesus came from the royal line (Luke 2:4; Acts 2:29-30; Rom. 1:3; 2 Tim . 2:8; Rev. 22:16). The Davidic covenant mandates that a literal Millennial Kingdom, led by the Messiah, Jesus Christ, must occur in the eschatological future.

Land Covenant

God instituted the land covenant with the Jewish people, the descendants of Abraham, Isaac, and Jacob (Gen 12:7; Deut. 30:1-5). Certain theologians improperly refer to the land covenant as the Palestinian covenant; but the term Palestinian is never used in Scripture. The land covenant involves several specific promises specifically given to the Jewish people, not the Church (the body of Christ), as the covenant, replacement, and supersessionist theologians suggest. First, God promised to regather the dispersed Jewish people from all over the world (Deut. 20:3-4). Second, God promises to give the land that he promised the patriarchs, to the regathered Jewish people, which is the land of Israel (Deut. 30:5). Third, once the regathering takes place, Moses prophesied that God shall greatly multiply the people, and they will love the Lord their God. This event has not occurred. However, following the rapture of the Church and the completion of the Tribulation period, God's promise to the Jewish people shall be fulfilled during Christ's Millennial Kingdom.[169]

New Covenant

The New Covenant, by definition, must replace the old covenant, better started as the Mosaic covenant. Several important aspects exist in the New Covenant. As with the previous three covenants, God specifically made the New Covenant with "Israel and the house of Judah," the Jewish people (Jer. 31:31).[170] God promised in the New Covenant to put His "law in their minds," He shall be the God of the people of Israel, and they shall be His people (Jer. 31:33).

---

[169] Fruchtenbaum, 425.
[170] Larry D. Pettegrew, "The New Covenant," *TMSJ* (Fall 1999), 251-252.

The wonderful promise included that all people shall know the Lord (Jer. 31:34). The eschatological people of Israel shall all speak the Hebrew language (Jer. 31:23), a phenomenon that has already begun in Israel. God strongly emphasized that this eschatological covenant with the Jewish people shall find fulfillment in the Millennial Kingdom by stating that if the sun, moon and stars depart, then the covenant becomes void (Jer. 31:35-36). That statement from God mandates the eschatological Millennial Kingdom, where Jesus Christ shall rule.

Inauguration of the Messianic Kingdom

Scripture unequivocally mandates that the literal one-thousand-year, eschatological, theocratic, Millennial Kingdom of the Lord Jesus Christ shall occur. In the Olivet Discourse, Jesus specifically outlined the events leading to His second coming, as He prepares to inaugurate His kingdom.

> Immediately after the tribulation of those days the sun will be darkened, and the moon will not give its light; the stars will fall from heaven, and the powers of the heavens will be shaken. Then the sign of the Son of Man will appear in heaven, and then all the tribes of the earth will mourn, and they will see the Son of Man coming on the clouds of heaven with power and great glory. And He will send His angels with a great sound of a trumpet, and they will gather together His elect from the four winds, from one end of heaven to the other. (Matt. 24:29-31)

The theocratic, messianic, Millennial Kingdom, shall come to fulfillment after the second advent of Jesus Christ to earth. Certain dispensational theologians outline the events regarding the return of Jesus as following the sequence of the fall Jewish feasts. Jesus Christ already followed the exact pattern of the spring feasts in His death on Passover, His burial on the Feast of Unleavened Bread, His ascension on the Feast of Firstfruits, and the coming of the promised Holy Spirit fifty days after Passover on Pentecost. Therefore, it is anticipated that Jesus will return to earth at His second advent on the Feast of Trumpets or Rosh Hashanah. At that time He will judge the surviving Gentile nations, living Jews, Satan, Antichrist, and the False Prophet during the Feast of Yom Kippur, or the Day of

Atonement, and finally, Jesus will officially inaugurate the Millennial Kingdom on the Feast of Tabernacles or Sukkot.[171]

The Participants in the Millennium

In addition to the glorified Church Age saints, the participants in the Millennium include the resurrected Old Testament saints in their glorified bodies (Dan 12:2), and all of those included in the *First Resurrection*, which includes those martyred during the seven-year Tribulation, and all of the Old Testament saints (Rev 20:4). In the Olivet Discourse, the Lord Jesus stated that a group of living believers in the Lord shall enter the Millennial Kingdom in their human bodies. Jesus also explained, concerning the remaining living people in the world, that at the conclusion of the battle of Armageddon, He shall gather all nations before Him, and judge each person regarding their belief in the Messiah. The Lord forbids those who failed to believe on Him entrance into the Millennial Kingdom. The Lord will cast the unbelievers, whom He also calls "goats", into the eternal lake of fire (Matt. 25:41). All believers in the Messiah, who are living at the end of the Tribulation, shall be ushered into the Millennial Kingdom in their human body. Jesus refers to this group as His sheep. Jesus states, regarding His sheep, "Then the King will say to those on His right hand, 'Come, you blessed of My Father, inherit the kingdom prepared for you from the foundation of the world" (Matt. 25:34).[172]

The Powerful Theocratic Ruler

The powerful theocratic Ruler, the Lord Jesus Christ takes His rightful place as the King of kings and Lord of lords in His Millennial Kingdom (Ps. 136:3; Isa. 9:6-7; 1 Tim. 6:15; Rev. 17:14; 20:4). Isaiah prophesied the future Millennial Kingdom when he pointed out that

---

[171] Jimmy DeYoung, *Revelation: A Chronology*, (Chattanooga: Shofar Communications, 2010), 134-137.
[172] John F. Walvoord, *The Millennial Kingdom* (Grand Rapids: Zondervan, 1959), 317.

the One who would be born as a child, referencing the birth of Jesus Christ, would one day literally bring it to fulfillment.

> For unto us a Child is born, Unto us a Son is given; And the government will be upon His shoulder. And His name will be called Wonderful, Counselor, Mighty God, Everlasting Father, Prince of Peace. ⁷Of the increase of His government and peace There will be no end, Upon the throne of David and over His kingdom, To order it and establish it with judgment and justice From that time forward, even forever. The zeal of the Lord of hosts will perform this. (Isaiah 9:6-7).

The Productive and Peaceful Environment

The Millennial Kingdom marks the return of life spans that have the potential to last one thousand years. Methuselah lived nine hundred and sixty-nine years. He is the oldest person ever recorded on earth (Gen. 5:27). Those who enter the Millennial Kingdom in non-glorified bodies shall live the entire one thousand years, and produce offspring. The children of those entering the Millennium will inherit the sin nature (Rom. 5:12), and they must make a conscious decision to accept the Lord Jesus Christ as their Savior (Rom. 10:13). Isaiah discusses this issue when stating: "No more shall an infant from there live but a few days, Nor an old man who has not fulfilled his days; For the child shall die one hundred years old, But the sinner being one hundred years old shall be accursed" (Isa. 65:20). Only one who rejects the Lord Jesus Christ and chooses to live a sinful lifestyle has the potential to die during the Millennial Kingdom.[173] Zechariah prophesied that the old men and women of "great age" will watch the children playing on the streets of Jerusalem (Zech 8:4-5).

The peaceful land of Israel shall produce great crops and the people will live without the fear of crime. "They shall build houses and inhabit them; They shall plant vineyards and eat their fruit. They shall not build and another inhabit; They shall not plant and another eat; For as the days of a tree, so shall be the days of My people, And My elect shall long enjoy the work of their hands. They shall not labor in vain, nor bring forth children for trouble; for they shall be the descendants of the blessed of the Lord, And their offspring with them" (Isa. 65:21-23).

---

[173] Ibid., 318-319.

The effects of God's curse on the earth shall be removed during the magnificent Millennial Kingdom. Isaiah beautifully describes the Kingdom's peaceful nature where the wolf and the lamb will lie down together, the leopard will not attack the goat for food, the lions will not attack the inferior animals for food, and amazingly, Isaiah states that a child will walk among the once wild carnivorous animals, and not suffer harm (Isa.11:6-8; 65:23-25). Isaiah specifically stated, "They shall not hurt nor destroy in all my holy mountain: for the earth shall be full of the knowledge of the LORD, as the waters cover the sea" (Isa. 11:9).[174] Zechariah also prophesied regarding the eschatological guarantee, "¹And *men* shall dwell in it, and there shall be no more utter destruction; but Jerusalem shall be safely inhabited" (Zech 14:11).

The Practice of Worship

The Millennial Kingdom marks a massive change regarding the worship of the Lord Jesus Christ. When Jesus Christ returns to establish His theocratic rule, He will build His beautiful Millennial Temple (Zech 6:12-15). The details of the Millennial Temple and the sacrificial system are found in Ezekiel 40-48. Nothing else in history fits Ezekiel's descriptions of Jerusalem and the Temple. In summary, the prophet Ezekiel provided a very detailed account of the greatly expanded dimensions of the Temple Mount, the Millennial Temple. Ezekiel also details the specific implements of the Temple worship, the sacrifices performed during the Millennium, the specified division of the land among the Jewish people, and the large expanded sacred area specific for the Temple Mount and the Temple.[175]

Worshipping the Messiah during the Millennium is mandatory. The prophet Zechariah clearly recorded that all of those who enter the Millennium, from all nations, shall make the pilgrimage to Jerusalem every year to "worship the King, the LORD of hosts, and to keep the feast of tabernacles" (Zech. 14:16). God made it clear that He will sanction those who refuse to come to Jerusalem

---

[174] Geoffrey W. Grogan, "Isaiah," ed. Frank E. Gaebelein, in *The Expositor's Bible Commentary* (Grand Rapids: Zondervan, 1986), 88-91.

[175] Ralph H. Alexander, "Ezekiel" ed. Frank E. Gaebelein, in *The Expositor's Bible Commentary* (Grand Rapids: Zondervan, 1986), 943-952.

and worship the Lord by withholding rain from their specific land (Zech. 14:17). Scripture states that all the ends of the world will remember the Lord, turn to Him, and worship Him (Ps. 22:27). The masses of people shall say, "Come, and let us go up to the mountain of the LORD, and to the house of the God of Jacob; and he will teach us of his ways, and we will walk in his paths: for the law shall go forth of Zion, and the word of the LORD from Jerusalem" (Micah. 4:2).

Theological Challenges

Numerous theologians disagree with the dispensational interpretation of Scripture. The most abhorrent results of the detractors regard the conclusions of the covenant, replacement, and supersessionist theologians. In addition, the recent start of progressive dispensational theology presents a dangerous attempt to synchronize dispensational and covenant theology, resulting in highly suspect conclusions.

Covenant Theology

The covenant theological construct interprets the Scriptures using an allegorical and spiritualization of the Scriptures. Roy Zuck, a dispensational theologian, strongly opposed the allegorical and spiritualizing of Scripture, as the conclusions result in arbitrary exegesis, and depend on the interpreter's imagination, resulting in an obscure interpretation.[176] The covenant construct denies the literal prophetic timeline presented in Scripture, thereby negating the literal Rapture of the Church (1 Thess. 4:`13-18; 1 Cor. 15:50-54) as the next major event in God's calendar, the eschatological literal seven-year Tribulation period as expressed in a plethora of Old Testament and New Testament texts (Representative passages: Isa. 2:12; 13:6-9; Joel 1:1:15; 2:1, 11, 31; 3:14; Zeph. 1:7, 14; Zech. 14:1; Dan. 9:27; Matt. 24:4-28 ; 2 Thess. 2; Rev. 6-18) and the Millennial Kingdom (Rev. 20:1-7), resulting in an amillennial or postmillennial position. Renald Showers concluded that only the premillennial view of the Millennium agrees with the Kingdom of God concept, specifically as outlined in Scripture. Amillennialism rejects the concept of the restoration of the Theocratic Kingdom to this present

---

[176] Roy Zuck, *Basic Bible Interpretation* (Colorado Springs: David C. Cook, 1991), 45-46.

earth. Postmillennialism concludes that Jesus returns at His second coming after the Church restores the earth to a Christ-like condition through human effort.[177]

The most dangerous aspect of covenant theology regards denying the Scriptural fact that God made direct eschatological covenants with Israel, the Jewish people, which must come to fulfillment, including the Abrahamic, Land, Davidic, and New covenants, resulting in replacement and supersessionist theology.[178] Michael Vlach pointed out three specific issues that lead to the faulty replacement or supersessionist position. First, the increasing Gentile composition of the first-century church; second, the church's wrong perception of the destruction of Jerusalem in A.D. 70 and 135; and third, a hermeneutical methodology of interpretation that allowed the church to appropriate promises made specific to Israel. "Together these factors contributed to the belief that the church had permanently replaced Israel as God's people."[179]

Denying the dispensational hermeneutic, including the historical, contextual, grammatical, and literal interpretation of Scripture, and embracing the allegorizing of the Bible, results in the heresy of replacement and supersessionist theology. They falsely and unequivocally state that Israel, and all of the promises God made to the Jewish people, are no longer applicable to the Jewish people, but are now all transferred, one hundred percent, to the Church. Therefore, the Church "replaces" and "supersedes" Israel, a conclusion that contradicts Scripture.

The results of replacement and supersessionist theology include horrific anti-Semitic persecution of the Jewish people since the start of the Church Age. History is replete with the inhumane treatment of the Jewish people leading to the largest historical account of the attempted extermination of the Jewish people during the Holocaust, resulting in the murdering of six million individual Jewish people. It is strongly suggested that the dispensational theological construct properly interprets Scripture to prevent the horrific results of such inappropriate methods presented in covenant

---

[177] Ibid.

[178] See previous section in this paper "Positive Guarantee of the Messianic Kingdom."

[179] Michael J. Vlach, *Has the Church Replaced Israel* (Nashville: B&H Academic, 2010), 28-29.

theology. Rightly dividing the Scriptures into specific dispensational periods is an interpretive methodology mandated by God (Dan. 9:24-27; 2 Tim. 2:15).

Progressive Dispensationalism

The final interpretive challenge that recently appeared in a newer theological school of thought has to do with the Progressive Dispensational theological construct. The main proponents and authors associated with Progressive Dispensational theology include Darrell Bock, Craig Blaising, and Robert Saucy. The issue related to the subject matter of "the Kingdom: now, or yet to come," forces the warning regarding the Progressive Dispensational interpretation of the "kingdom." The concept of the kingdom to the Progressive Dispensational theologian is that the kingdom is here, but will not come to its fullest extent until Jesus returns, stated as the "here, but not yet." Saucy states, "Only certain dimensions of it (*kingdom*) came through the first advent of Christ and are present today." He further concluded that the kingdom is "primarily future," and therefore Christians should pray currently for the kingdom to come as Jesus taught His Jewish disciples to pray. [180]

Bock and Blaising add to the argument that the kingdom is partially in existence during the Church Age. They added the concept that the kingdom exists in mystery form, during the current Church Age, with the King positioned in heaven, and the citizens of the kingdom currently on earth. When the Lord Jesus returns to the earth, then the kingdom comes to its "fullness."[181] Simply stated, progressive dispensationalism walks a fine line between covenant and dispensational theology, by accepting the covenant position that the kingdom currently is in effect yet also embracing a literal Tribulation and Millennium.

Conclusion

A proper comprehension of God's prophetic timeline, as found in the Scriptures, reveals why the development of AI and transhumanism will likely play a major role in the coming seven-year Tribulation period. The god of this world, Satan (2 Cor. 4:4), who is

---

[180] Robert L, Saucy, The Case for Progressive Dispensationalism, The Interface Between Dispensational & Non-Dispensational Theology (Grand Rapids: Zondervan, 1993), 98, 101.

[181] Craig A. Blaising, *Progressive Dispensationalism* Grand Rapids: Baker Books, 1993), 254.

the great deceiver and liar (John 8:44), will incorporate every possible method to control the world. God allows him extreme latitude to corrupt the entire world system for seven years (Rev. 13). Satan will accomplish God's sovereign will, even though Satan's goal is to destroy God and His followers.

God's desire during the catastrophic Tribulation is to purge the earth of all that is evil, so that when the Lord Jesus Christ returns bodily to this earth with His saints, Jesus enters a purified earth, ready to receive Him as their King. That is exactly what God will accomplish, despite the arsenal of weapons that Satan is currently using, including technology, AI, transhumanism, and the de-evolution of democracy. Satan and his demonic army are currently using their influence to move the masses away from a biblical worldview to one which will one day embrace the likes of the Antichrist, who will bring to fulfillment the globalists' dream of the one-world government, economy, and religion. Satan, Antichrist, the false prophet, and all throughout history who have attempted to thwart God's sovereign plan, will realize all too late, that everything they attempted to accomplish will end in eternal torment, and accomplish exactly what God intended since eternity past.
Here we stand; we cannot, we must not be moved!

The devil, who deceived them, was cast into the lake of fire and brimstone where the beast and the false prophet are. And they will be tormented day and night forever and ever.

Revelation 20:10

And He said to me, "It is done! I am the Alpha and the Omega, the Beginning and the End. I will give of the fountain of the water of life freely to him who thirsts. He who overcomes shall inherit all things, and I will be his God and he shall be My son. But the cowardly, unbelieving, abominable, murderers, sexually immoral, sorcerers, idolaters, and all liars shall have their part in the lake which burns with fire and brimstone, which is the second death."

Revelation 21:6-8

APPENDIX A[182]

The following question was presented to ChatGPT.
"What are the top uses of Artificial Intelligence?"

ChatGPT responded with the following answer.

Here are 84 uses of Artificial Intelligence (AI):

1. Virtual personal assistants (e.g., Siri, Alexa)
2. Natural language processing for chatbots and customer support
3. Recommendation systems (e.g., personalized product recommendations)
4. Fraud detection and prevention in banking and finance
5. Autonomous vehicles and self-driving cars
6. Image and object recognition in computer vision
7. Speech recognition and transcription services
8. Sentiment analysis for social media monitoring
9. Predictive maintenance for machinery and equipment
10. Healthcare diagnostics and medical image analysis
11. Financial market analysis and trading algorithms
12. Personalized news and content curation
13. Virtual reality and augmented reality applications
14. Cybersecurity threat detection and prevention
15. Supply chain and logistics optimization
16. Energy consumption optimization and smart grids
17. Robotics and automation in manufacturing
18. Language translation and interpretation services
19. Virtual try-on for e-commerce and fashion
20. Content generation for news and articles
21. Drug discovery and development in pharmaceuticals
22. Facial recognition for security and authentication
23. Gaming and interactive entertainment experiences
24. Customer sentiment analysis and feedback analysis
25. Precision agriculture and crop monitoring
26. Human resources and talent acquisition
27. Speech synthesis and voice assistants

---

[182] OpenAI. (2023, June 14). What are the top 99 uses of Artificial Intelligence? [Response to user query]. In ChatGPT (Version 3.5) [Computer software]. OpenAI. Retrieved from [URL of this conversation]

28. Chatbot-driven customer service
29. Personalized marketing and targeted advertising
30. Social media monitoring and trend analysis
31. Language tutoring and educational applications
32. Weather prediction and climate modeling
33. Object detection and tracking in surveillance systems
34. Quality control and defect detection in manufacturing
35. Noise cancellation and audio enhancement
36. Virtual assistants for scheduling and productivity
37. Personalized fitness and health monitoring
38. Recommendation systems for online streaming services
39. Document analysis and text summarization
40. Sentiment analysis for customer feedback
41. Wildlife conservation and monitoring
42. Disaster response and emergency management
43. Smart home automation and IoT integration
44. Inventory management and demand forecasting
45. Emotional AI for mental health support
46. Legal research and contract analysis
47. Speech-to-text services for transcription
48. Facial expression analysis and emotion detection
49. Personalized learning platforms and adaptive education
50. Autonomous drones and aerial surveillance
51. Gesture recognition for human-computer interaction
52. Data analytics and insights generation
53. Fraud detection in insurance claims
54. Predictive analytics for business forecasting
55. Biometric identification and authentication
56. Virtual assistants for elderly and disability care
57. Language understanding and sentiment analysis in customer service
58. Traffic management and congestion prediction
59. E-commerce product search and recommendation
60. Real-time language translation for communication
61. Smart city infrastructure and management
62. Conversational AI for language learning
63. Patient monitoring and health diagnostics
64. Event prediction and anomaly detection in IoT systems
65. Retail inventory optimization and shelf management
66. Music composition and generation

67. Customer churn prediction and retention strategies
68. Fraud detection in credit card transactions
69. Chatbot-driven mental health support
70. Smart grid optimization and energy distribution
71. Sports analytics and performance tracking
72. Employee sentiment analysis and engagement measurement
73. Personalized travel recommendations and planning
74. Predictive maintenance for aviation and aerospace
75. Robotics in healthcare and surgery
76. Insurance underwriting and risk assessment
77. Art creation and painting
78. Smart advertising and dynamic pricing
79. Environmental monitoring and conservation
80. Data-driven farming and livestock management
81. Online learning platforms with adaptive content
82. Speech analytics for call center quality monitoring
83. Content moderation and filtering in social media
84. Disease outbreak prediction and response planning

APPENDIX B[183]

The following question was presented to ChatGPT.

"What are the top 100 concepts regarding artificial intelligence?"

ChatGPT responded with the following answer.

Certainly! Here are 100 top concepts regarding Artificial Intelligence (AI):

1. Machine Learning
2. Deep Learning
3. Neural Networks
4. Natural Language Processing (NLP)
5. Computer Vision
6. Reinforcement Learning
7. Supervised Learning
8. Unsupervised Learning
9. Semi-supervised Learning
10. Transfer Learning
11. Data Mining
12. Feature Extraction
13. Dimensionality Reduction
14. Ensemble Learning
15. Decision Trees
16. Support Vector Machines (SVM)
17. Genetic Algorithms
18. Bayesian Networks
19. Expert Systems
20. Knowledge Representation
21. Logical Reasoning
22. Cognitive Computing
23. Explainable AI (XAI)
24. Robotics
25. Swarm Intelligence
26. Fuzzy Logic
27. Pattern Recognition

---

[183]OpenAI. (2023, June 14). "What are the top 100 concepts regarding artificial intelligence?"[Response to user query]. In ChatGPT (Version 3.5) [Computer software]. OpenAI. Retrieved from [URL of this conversation]

28. Predictive Analytics
29. Data Preprocessing
30. Overfitting and Underfitting
31. Bias and Variance
32. Model Evaluation and Selection
33. Hyperparameter Tuning
34. Loss Functions
35. Convolutional Neural Networks (CNN)
36. Recurrent Neural Networks (RNN)
37. Generative Adversarial Networks (GANs)
38. Autoencoders
39. Word Embeddings
40. Sentiment Analysis
41. Speech Recognition
42. Image Segmentation
43. Reinforcement Learning Algorithms (e.g., Q-Learning)
44. Ethics and Responsible AI
45. Explainability and Transparency in AI
46. AI Safety and Risk Mitigation
47. Human-AI Collaboration
48. AI Governance and Regulation
49. AI Bias and Fairness
50. AI in Healthcare
51. Swarm Robotics
52. Natural Language Generation
53. Active Learning
54. Anomaly Detection
55. Collaborative Filtering
56. Data Augmentation
57. Data Imputation
58. Data Labeling
59. Data Visualization
60. Ensemble Methods
61. Evolutionary Computation
62. Face Recognition
63. Generative Models
64. Graph Neural Networks
65. Hyperparameter Optimization
66. Instance-based Learning
67. Interpretability in AI

68. Knowledge Graphs
69. Markov Decision Processes
70. Multi-Agent Systems
71. Object Detection
72. Online Learning
73. Optimization Algorithms
74. Principal Component Analysis (PCA)
75. Quantum Computing and AI
76. Recommender Systems
77. Robotic Process Automation (RPA)
78. Scene Understanding
79. Self-Supervised Learning
80. Sequence-to-Sequence Models
81. Social Robotics
82. Sparse Coding
83. Time Series Analysis
84. Transfer Learning for NLP
85. Uncertainty Quantification
86. Variational Autoencoders
87. Weak Supervision
88. Zero-shot Learning
89. Active Vision
90. Adversarial Examples
91. Attention Mechanisms
92. Automated Planning
93. Cognitive Robotics
94. Common Sense Reasoning
95. Counterfactual Reasoning
96. Deep Reinforcement Learning
97. Emotion AI
98. Explainable Reinforcement Learning
99. Federated Learning
100. Reinforcement Learning in Robotics

These concepts cover a broad range of topics in the field of AI and provide a comprehensive overview of its fundamental principles and applications. It's important to note that AI is a rapidly evolving field, and new concepts and techniques continue to emerge over time.

APPENDIX C[184]

The following question was presented to ChatGPT.

Describe in detail how Siri works.

ChatGPT responded with the following answer.

Siri is a virtual personal assistant developed by Apple that uses artificial intelligence and natural language processing to provide voice-activated assistance and perform various tasks on Apple devices. Here's a detailed overview of how Siri works:

1. Speech Recognition: When you activate Siri by saying "Hey Siri" or pressing the Siri button, the device's microphone captures your voice and converts it into digital audio.
2. Audio Processing: The audio data is processed to remove background noise and enhance voice clarity. Siri's algorithms analyze the audio waveform to identify speech patterns and separate it from other sounds.
3. Natural Language Understanding (NLU): Siri uses NLU techniques to comprehend the meaning and intent behind your spoken words. The speech input is transformed into a structured representation that Siri's system can interpret and process.
4. Intent Recognition: Siri analyzes the interpreted input to identify the user's intent and determine the appropriate action to take. It recognizes keywords, phrases, and context clues to understand user commands or queries.
5. Query Processing: Once the intent is recognized, Siri generates a query based on the user's request. The query is formulated to retrieve relevant information or trigger specific actions. For example, if you ask Siri about the weather, it formulates a query to retrieve weather data from a reliable source.
6. Data Retrieval: Siri connects to various data sources, including online services and databases, to fetch the information requested by the user. It may access weather

---

[184] OpenAI. (2023, June 14). "Describe in detail how Siri works." [Response to user query]. In ChatGPT (Version 3.5) [Computer software]. OpenAI. Retrieved from [URL of this conversation]

APIs, search engines, mapping services, or other relevant sources to gather data.
7. Knowledge Base: Siri has a vast knowledge base that contains information on a wide range of topics. It leverages this knowledge base to provide answers to factual queries, such as general knowledge questions, sports scores, or historical facts.
8. Personalization: Siri can access data and preferences stored on your device, such as contacts, calendar events, and app settings. This enables Siri to provide personalized responses and perform tasks specific to your needs. For example, it can schedule appointments, send messages, or make calls on your behalf.
9. Task Execution: After processing your request and retrieving relevant data, Siri performs the requested task or provides the information you need. This can include setting reminders, sending emails, playing music, providing directions, or controlling device settings.
10. Continuous Learning: Siri incorporates machine learning algorithms to improve its performance over time. It learns from user interactions and feedback, adapting to individual preferences and refining its understanding and response capabilities.

It's important to note that Siri's functionalities and the underlying technology may evolve over time as Apple continues to enhance and update its virtual assistant. The specific algorithms, models, and processes utilized by Siri may vary based on device capabilities, operating system versions, and privacy settings.

Free Research Preview. ChatGPT may produce inaccurate information about people, places, or facts. ChatGPT May 24 Version

APPENDIX D[185]

The following is the speech given by President Joe Biden on November 2, 2022. The content of the speech does not necessarily represent the position of the author of this book.

Good evening, everyone. Just a few days ago a little before 2:30 a.m. in the morning, a man smashed the back window and broke into the home of the speaker of the House of Representatives, the third highest-ranking official in America. He carried in his backpack zip-ties, duct tape, rope, and a hammer.

As he told the police, he had come looking for Nancy Pelosi to take her hostage, to interrogate her, to threaten to break her kneecaps. But she wasn't there. Her husband, my friend Paul Pelosi, was home alone. The assailant tried to take Paul hostage. He woke him up and he wanted to tie him up. The assailant ended up using a hammer to smash Paul's skull. Thankfully, by the grace of god, Paul survived. All this happened after the assault, and it just – it's hard to even say.

After the assailant entered the home asking "Where's Nancy? Where's Nancy?" Those are the very same words used by the mob when they stormed the United States Capitol on January the 6th, when they broke windows, kicked in the doors, brutally attacked law enforcement, roamed the corridors hunting for officials, and erected gallows to hang the former Vice President Mike Pence. It was an enraged mob that had been whipped up into a frenzy by a president repeating over and over again the big lie: that the election of 2020 had been stolen. It's a lie that fueled the dangerous rise in political violence and voter intimidation over the past two years.

Even before January the 6th, we saw election officials and election workers in a number of states subject to menacing calls, physical threats, even threats to their very lives. In Georgia, for example, Republican secretary of state and his family were subjected to death threats because he refused to break the law and give into the defeated president's demand to just find him 11,780 votes. Just find me 11,780 votes. Election workers, like Shaye Moss and her mother Ruby Freeman, were harassed and threatened just because they had the courage to do their job and stand up for the truth, to stand up for our democracy.

---

[185] "Remarks by President Biden on Standing up for Democracy," White House, November 3, 2022, https://www.whitehouse.gov/briefing-room/speeches-remarks/2022/11/03/remarks-by-president-biden-on-standing-up-for-democracy/, accessed August 28, 2023.

This institution, this intimidation, this violence against Democrats, Republicans, and nonpartisan officials just doing their jobs, are the consequence of lies told for power and profit. Lies of conspiracy and malice, lies repeated over and over to generate a cycle of anger, hate, vitriol and even violence. In this moment, we have to confront those lies with the truth. The very future of our nation depends on it.

My fellow Americans, we're facing a defining moment. An inflexion point. We must with one overwhelming, unified voice speak as a country and say there's no place, no place for voter intimidation or political violence in America. Whether it's directed at Democrats or Republicans. No place, period. No place ever. I speak today near Capitol Hill, near the US Capitol, the citadel of our democracy.

I know there's a lot of stake in these midterm elections, from our economy, to the safety of our streets, to our personal freedoms, to the future of health care and Social Security, Medicare. It's all important. But we'll have our differences, we'll have our difference of opinion. And that's what it's supposed to be.

But there's something else at stake: democracy itself. I'm not the only one who sees it. Recent polls have shown an overwhelming majority of Americans believe our democracy is at risk, that our democracy's under threat. They too see that democracy is on the ballot this year, and they're deeply concerned about it.

So today I appeal to all Americans, regardless of party, to meet this moment of national and generational importance. We must vote knowing what's at stake and not just the policy of the moment, but institutions that have held us together as we've sought a more perfect union are also at stake. We must vote knowing who we have been, what we're at risk of becoming.

Look, my fellow Americans, the old expression "freedom is not free," it requires constant vigilance. From the very beginning, nothing has been guaranteed about democracy in America. Every generation has had to defend it, protect it, preserve it, choose it. That's what democracy is. It's a choice, a decision of the people, by the people, and for the people. The issue couldn't be clearer, in my view. We the people must decide whether we will have fair and free elections, and every vote counts. We the people must decide whether we're going to sustain a republic where reality is accepted, the law is obeyed, and your vote is truly sacred. We the people must decide whether the rule of law will prevail or whether we will allow the dark forces and thirst for power put ahead of the principles that have long guided us.

You know, American democracy is under attack because the defeated former president of the United States refused to accept the results of the 2020 election. If he refuses to accept the will of the people, refuses to accept the fact that he lost, he has abused his power and put the loyalty to himself before loyalty to the Constitution. And he's made a big lie, an article of faith in the MAGA Republican party, the minority of that party. The great irony about the 2020 election is that it's the most attacked election in our history. And yet, and yet, there's no election in our history that we can be more certain of its results. Every legal challenge that could have been brought, was brought. Every recount that could have been undertaken, was undertaken. Every recount confirmed the results. Wherever fact or evidence had been demanded, the big lie has been proven to be just that, a big lie. Every single time.

Yet now, extreme MAGA Republicans aim to question not only the legitimacy of past elections, but elections being held now and into the future. The extreme MAGA element of the republican party, which is a minority of that party, as I said earlier, but it's its driving force. It's trying to succeed where they failed in 2020, to suppress the right of voters and subvert the electoral system itself. That means denying your right to vote and deciding whether your vote even counts. Instead of waiting until an election is over, they're starting well before it. They're starting now. They've emboldened violence and intimidation of voters and election officials. It's estimated that there are more than 300 election deniers on the ballot all across America this year. We can't ignore the impact this is having on our country. It's damaging, it's corrosive, and it's destructive. And I want to be very clear, this is not about me, it's about all of us. It's about what makes America, America. It's about the durability of our democracy.

For democracies are more than a form of government. They're a way of being, a way of seeing the world, a way that defines who we are, what we believe, why we do what we do. Democracy is simply that fundamental. We must, in this moment, dig deep within ourselves and recognize that we can't take democracy for granted any longer. With democracy on the ballot, we have to remember these first principles. Democracy means the rule of the people, not the rule of monarchs or the moneyed, but the rule of the people.

Autocracy is the opposite of democracy. It means the rule of one, one person, one interest, one ideology, one party. To state the obvious, the lives of billions of people, from antiquity till now, have been shaped by the battle between these competing forces, between the aspirations of the many and the greed and power of the few, between the people's right for self-determination, and the self-seeking autocrat, between the dreams of a democracy and the appetites of an autocracy. What we're doing now is going to determine whether democracy will long endure and, in my view, is the biggest of questions, whether the American system that prizes the individual bends towards justice and depends on the rule of law, whether that system will prevail. This is the struggle we're now in, a struggle for democracy, a struggle for decency and dignity, a struggle for prosperity and progress, a struggle for the very soul of America itself.

Make no mistake, democracy is on the ballot for all of us. We must remember that democracy is a covenant. We need to start looking out for each other again, seeing ourselves as we the people, not as entrenched enemies. This is a choice we can make. Disunion and chaos are not inevitable. There's been anger before in America. There's been division before in America. But we've never given up on the American experiment, and we can't do that now. The remarkable thing about American democracy is this: just enough of us on just enough occasions have chosen not to dismantle democracy, but to preserve democracy. We must choose that path again. Because democracy is on the ballot, we have to remember that even in our darkest moments, there are fundamental values and beliefs that unite us as Americans, and they must unite us now. What are they?

Well, I think, first, we believe the vote in America's sacred, to be honored, not denied, respected, not dismissed, counted, not ignored. A vote is not a partisan tool to be counted when it helps your candidates and tossed aside when it doesn't. Second, we must, with an overwhelming voice, stand against political violence and voter intimidation, period. Stand up and speak against it. We don't settle our differences, America, with a riot, a mob, or a bullet, or a hammer. We settle them peacefully at the ballot box.

We have to be honest with ourselves, though. We have to face this problem. We can't turn away from it. We can't pretend it's just going to solve itself. There's an alarming rise in the number of our people in this country condoning political violence, or simply remain silent because silence is complicity. To the disturbing rise of voter intimidation, the pernicious tendency to excuse political violence, or at least, try to explain it away. We can't allow this sentiment to grow. We must confront it head on now. It has to stop now.

I believe the voices excusing or calling for violence and intimidation are a distinct minority in America. But they're loud and they are determined. We have to be more determined. All of us who reject political violence and voter intimidation, and I believe that's the overwhelming majority of the American people, all of us must unite to make it absolutely clear that violence and intimidation have no place in America.

And third, we believe in democracy. That's who we are as Americans. I know it isn't easy. Democracy's imperfect. It always has been. But you're all called to defend it now, now. History and common sense tell us that liberty, opportunity, and justice thrive in a democracy, not in an autocracy.

At our best, America's not a zero-sum society – or for you to succeed, someone else has to fail. A promise in America is big enough, for everyone to succeed. Every generation, opening the door of opportunity just a little bit wider. Every generation, including those who've been excluded before. We believe we should leave no one behind, because each one of us is a child of god, and every person, every person is sacred. If that's true, then every person's rights must be sacred as well. Individual dignity, individual worth, individual determination. That's America, that's democracy, and that's what we have to defend.

Look, even as I speak here tonight, 27 million people have already cast their ballot in the midterm elections. Millions more will cast their ballots in the final days leading up to November the 9th – 8th, excuse me. And for the first time, this is the first time since the national election of 2020, once again we're seeing record turnout all over the country. And that's good. We want Americans to vote.

We want every American's voice to be heard. Now we have to move the process forward. We know that more and more ballots are cast in early voting or by mail in America. We know that many states don't start counting those ballots until after the polls close on November 8th. That means in some cases we won't know the winner of the election for a few days – until a few days after the election. It takes time to count all legitimate ballots in a legal and orderly manner. It's always been important for citizens in the democracy to be informed and engaged. Now it's important for a citizen to be patient as well. That's how this is supposed to work.

This is also the first election since the events of January 6th, when the armed angry mob stormed the US Capitol. I wish I could say the assault on our democracy ended that day, but I cannot. As I stand here today, there are candidates running for every level of office in America, for governor, congress, attorney general, secretary of state, who won't commit, that will not commit to accepting the results of the election that they're running in. This is a path to chaos in America. It's unprecedented. It's unlawful, and it's un-American.

As I've said before, you can't love your country only when you win. This is no ordinary year. So I ask you to think long and hard about the moment we're in. In a typical year, we're often not faced with questions of whether the vote we cast will preserve democracy or put us at risk. But this year we are. This year I hope you'll make the future of our democracy an important part of your decision to vote and how you vote. I hope you'll ask a simple question of each candidate you might vote for. Will that person accept the legitimate will of the

American people and the people voting in his district or her district? Will that person accept the outcome of the election, win or lose? The answer to that question is vital. And, in my opinion, it should be decisive. And the answer to that question hangs in the future of the country we love so much, and the fate of the democracy that has made so much possible for us.

Too many people have sacrificed too much for too many years for us to walk away from the American project and democracy. Because we've endured our freedoms for so long, it's easy to think they'll always be with us no matter what. But that isn't true today. In our bones, we know democracy is at risk. But we also know this: it's within our power, each and every one of us, to preserve our democracy. And I believe we will. I think I know this country. I know we will.

You have the power, it's your choice, it's your decision, the fate of the nation, the fate of the soul of America lies where it always does – with the people, in your hands, in your heart, in your ballot. My fellow Americans, we'll meet this moment. We just need to remember who we are. We are the United States of America. There's nothing beyond our capacity if we do it together. May God bless you all. May God protect our troops. May God bless those standing guard over our democracy. Thank you, and Godspeed.

BIBLIOGRAPHY

Alexander, Ralph H. "Ezekiel" ed. Frank E. Gaebelein, in *The Expositor's Bible Commentary* (Grand Rapids: Zondervan, 1986), 943-952.

Anderson, Sir Robert. *The Coming Prince* (Grand Rapids, Kregel Publishing, 1975), 127-128.

Beacham, Roy E. "The Parables of the Kingdom" in *Dictionary of Premillennial Theology,* ed. Mal Couch (Grand Rapids: Kregel Publishing, 1996), 233-234.

Benware, Paul N. *Understanding End Times Prophecy* (Chicago: Moody Publishers, 2006), 306.

Bergman, Frank. "WEF Calls For AI To Rewrite Bible, Create 'Religions That Are Actually Correct', Slay News, June 10, 2023, https://www.sott.net/article/481178-WEF-calls-for-AI-to-rewrite-Bible-create-religions-that-are-actually-correct, accessed August 7, 2023.

Bishop, Lindsay. "Average Household Budget: How Much Does the Typical American Spend?" November 28, 2022, https://www.valuepenguin.com/average-household-budget#:~:text=The%20average%20American%20household%20spends%20%242%2C912%20per%20year%20on%20entertainment, accessed August 24, 2023.

Blaising, Craig A. *Progressive Dispensationalism* Grand Rapids: Baker Books, 1993), 254.

Blake, Aaron. "Democrats Are Now Going There On 'Stolen' Elections," The Washington Post, November 15, 2018, https://www.washingtonpost.com/politics/2018/11/15/democrats-are-now-going-there-stolen-elections/, accessed August 25, 2023.

Brown, Sara. "Machine Learning, Explained," MIT Management Sloan School, April 21, 2021, https://mitsloan.mit.edu/ideas-made-to-matter/machine-learning-explained, accessed August 4, 2023.

Burns, Ed. "Machine Learning," TechTarget, https://www.techtarget.com/searchenterpriseai/definition/machine-learning-ML?Offer=abt_pubpro_AI-Insider, accessed August 4,

2024.

Chriten, Gert. "Transhumanism – The technological evolution of humankind," GertChristen.org, March 31, 2021, https://www.gertchristen.org/transhumanism-rena-seiler/ accessed August 23, 2023.

Dahl, Robert A., David Froomkin, and Ian Shapiro, "History and Society Democracy," Encyclopedia Britannica, June 30, 2023, https://www.britannica.com/topic/democracy, accessed July 13, 2023.,

DeYoung, Jimmy. *Isaiah the Beloved Prophet*, Audio Series (Chattanooga: Prophecy Today, 2011). CD 3, Track 2.

_____. *Revelation: A Chronology*, (Chattanooga: Shofar Communications, 2010), 134-137.

_____. *Sound the Trumpets* (Chattanooga: Shofar Communications, 2000), 12-13.

Emmanuel, Rachel. "An AI Program is Pretending to be Jesus and Thousands of Lost Young People Are Flocking to It," June 15, 2023, https://www.westernjournal.com/ai-program-pretending-jesus-thousands-lost-young-people-flocking/, accessed August 6, 2023.

Feger, Arielle. AI spending will jump to $154 billion worldwide in 2023, Insider Intelligence, April 19, 2023, https://www.insiderintelligence.com/content/ai-spending-will-jump-billion-worldwide-2023, accessed August 15, 2023.

Flynn, Jack. "35+ Alarming Automation & Job Loss Statistics [2023]: Are Robots, Machines, And Ai Coming For Your Job?" Zippia, June 8, 2023, accessed August 15, 2023.

Fruchtenbaum, Arnold G. *The Footsteps of the Messiah* (San Antonio: Ariel Ministries, 2004), 420.

Grad, Peter. "AI Jesus Writes Bible-Inspired Verse, Tech Xplore, September 2, 2020, https://techxplore.com/news/2020-09-ai-jesus-bible-inspired-verse.html, accessed August 6, 2023.

Grisanti, Michael A. "The Davidic Covenant," *TMSJ* (Fall 1999), 233.

Grogan, Geoffrey W. "Isaiah," ed. Frank E. Gaebelein, in *The Expositor's Bible Commentary* (Grand Rapids: Zondervan, 1986), 88-91.

Hindson, Edward "Battle of Armageddon," In *Dictionary of Premillennial Theology.* Editor Mal Couch. Grand Rapids: Kregel Publications, 1996. 56-57.

Iozzio, Corinne. "Scientists Prove That Telepathic Communication Is Within Reach," Smithsonian Magazine, October 2, 2014, https://www.smithsonianmag.com/innovation/scientists-prove-that-telepathic-communication-is-within-reach-180952868/, accessed August 23, 2023.

Lloreda, Claudia López. "Nerve-Mimicking Device Gives 'Feeling' To Prosthetics," Science, July 28, 2023, https://www.science.org/content/article/nerve-mimicking-device-gives-feeling-prosthetics, accessed August 20, 2023.

Mann, Brian Brian. U.S. Drug Overdose Deaths Hit A Record In 2022 As Some States See A Big Surge, May 18, 2023, https://www.npr.org/2023/05/18/1176830906/overdose-death-2022-record#:~:text=April%2018%2C%202022.-,The%20latest%20federal%20data%20show%20more%20than%20109%2C000,in%202022%2C%20many%20from%20fentanyl, accessed August 16, 2023.

McClain, Alva J. *The Greatness of the Kingdom* (Winona Lake, BMH Books, 1974) 21.

Merritt, Alexandra. "Is AI a Threat to Christianity?" The Atlantic, February 3, 2017, https://www.theatlantic.com/technology/archive/2017/02/artificial-intelligence-christianity/515463/, accessed August 6, 2023.

Mirkes, Renée. "Transhumanist Medicine: Can We Direct Its Power to the Service of Human Dignity?" March 29, 2019, Linacre Quarterly, https://www.ncbi.nlm.nih.gov/pmc/articles/PMC6537347/, accessed August 23, 2023.

Muncaster, Phil. "Trojan Delilah Recruits Malicious Insiders Via Extortion," Infosecurity Magazine, July 18, 2016, https://www.infosecurity-magazine.com/news/trojan-delilah-recruits-malicious, accessed July 24, 2023.

Osmond, Candace. "Existential – Meaning & Definition," Grammarist, https://grammarist.com/usage/existential/accessed, August 17, 2023.

Ostberg, René. "transhumanism". Encyclopedia Britannica, 3 Nov. 2022, https://www.britannica.com/topic/transhumanism. Accessed 20 August 2023.

Pentecost, J. Dwight. "Daniel," in *The Bible Knowledge Commentary: An Exposition of the Scriptures*.

Punt, Dominic. "The World's Oldest People and Their Secrets to a Long Life," accessed August 8, 22, 2023.

Pettegrew, Larry D. "The New Covenant," *TMSJ* (Fall 1999), 251-252.

Price, J. Randall. "Old Testament References to the Tribulation," in *Dictionary of Premillennial Theology,* ed. Mal Couch (Grand rapids: Kregel Publishing, 1996) 412-413.

_____. "The Future Temple," in *Dictionary of Premillennial Theology,* ed. Mal Couch (Grand Rapids: Kregel Publishing, 1996), 404-405.

Ramm, Bernard. *Protestant Biblical Interpretation* (Grand Rapids: Baker Book House, 1970), 119, 136, 138.

Russell, Stuart. Human Compatible, Artificial Intelligence and the Problem of Control (New York; Penguin Books, 2020), 104.

Russell, Stuart and Peter Norvig Editors, *Artificial Intelligence, A Modern Approach* (Pearson India Education Services Private Limited, 2022), 1009.

Sailhamer, John H. "Genesis," ed. Frank E. Gaebelein, in *The Expositor's Bible Commentary* (Grand Rapids: Zondervan, 1990), 76.

Saucy, Robert L. The Case for Progressive Dispensationalism, The Interface Between Dispensational & Non-Dispensational Theology (Grand Rapids: Zondervan, 1993), 98, 101.

Shatzer, Jacob. *Transhumanism and the Image of God* (Downers Grove, ILL.; IVP Academic, 2019), 91.

Showers, Renald E. *There Really is a Difference! A Comparison of Covenant and Dispensational Theology* (Bellmawr: The Friends of Israel Gospel Ministry, Inc., 1990), 161.

Silas Queiroz, "The Cybersecurity In The Age Of Transhumanism" August 2, 2021, Linkedin, https://www.linkedin.com/pulse/cybersecurity-age-transhumanism-silas-queiroz, , accessed August 23, 2023.

Slick, Matt. What is Cerinthianism? CARM, June 18, 2014, https://carm.org/about-heresies/what-is-cerinthianism/, accessed August 26, 2023.

Smith, Mark. "Breakthroughs in Prosthetic Technology Promise Better Living Through Design," October 6, 2021, https://redshift.autodesk.com/articles/prosthetic-technology, accessed August 20, 2023.

Sterling, Toby. and Stephanie van den Berg, "Ukraine war shows urgency of military AI, Palantir CEO says," Reuters, February 15, 2023, https://www.reuters.com/technology/ukraine-war-shows-urgency-military-ai-palantir-ceo-says-2023-02-15/, accessed August 17, 2023.

Toussaint, Stanley D. *Behold the King, A Study of Matthew* (Portland, Multnomah, 1980), 241. Toussaint, Stanley D. *Behold the King, A Study of Matthew* (Portland, Multnomah, 1980), 241.

Ulmer, Alexandra and Anna Tong, "Deepfaking It: America's 2024 Election Collides With AI Boom," Reuters, May 30, 2023, https://www.reuters.com/world/us/deepfaking-it-americas-2024-election-collides-with-ai-boom-2023-05-30/?utm_source=Sailthru&utm_medium=Newsletter&utm_campaign=Daily-Briefing&utm_term=053023, accessed July 24, 2023.

Vlach, Michael J. *Has the Church Replaced Israel* (Nashville: B&H Academic, 2010), 28-29.

Walvoord, John F. *Daniel*, ed. Charles H. Dyer and Philip E. Rawley (Chicago: Moody Publishers, 2012), 80-83.

_____. *Every Prophecy of the Bible*, (David C. Cook, Colorado Springs, CO.: 2011), 7.

_____. *The Millennial Kingdom* (Grand Rapids: Zondervan, 1959), 317.

_____. "Revelation," in *The Bible Knowledge Commentary: An Exposition of the Scriptures*, ed. J. F. Walvoord and R. B. Zuck, vol. 2 (Wheaton, IL: Victor Books, 1985), 960.

Yang, Angela. 'AI Jesus' is giving gaming and breakup advice on a 24/7 Twitch stream, NBC News, June 14, 2023, https://www.nbcnews.com/tech/ai-jesus-twitch-stream-rcna89187, accessed August 7, 2023.

Zuck, Roy. *Basic Bible Interpretation* (Colorado Springs: David C. Cook, 1991), 45-46.

"Algorithm." Merriam-Webster.com Dictionary, Merriam-Webster, https://www.merriam-webster.com/dictionary/algorithm. Accessed 4 Aug. 2023.

"Bombing of Hiroshima and Nagasaki," History.com editors, November 18, 2009, https://www.history.com/topics/world-war-ii/bombing-of-hiroshima-and-nagasaki, accessed August 16, 2023.

"Democracy." MERRIAM-WEBSTER.COM DICTIONARY, Merriam-Webster, https://www.merriam-webster.com/dictionary/democracy. Accessed 13 Jul. 2023.

"Democracy or Republic: What's the difference?" MERRIAM-WEBSTER.COM DICTIONARY, Merriam-Webster, https://www.merriam-webster.com/grammar/democracy-and-republic, accessed August 25, 2023.

"Disciple," Merriam-Webster.com Dictionary, s.v., https://www.merriam-webster.com/dictionary/disciples, accessed August 21, 2023.

"Elon Musk Tells Tucker Potential Dangers of Hyper-Intelligent AI," Fox News, https://youtu.be/a2ZBEC16yH4, accessed August 11, 2023.

"Ethics Explainer: Post-Humanism," The Ethics Center, February 22, 2018, https://ethics.org.au/ethics-explainer-post-humanism/, accessed August 21, 2023.

"Google Engineer on AI Dangers," YouTube, https://youtu.be/kgCUn4fQTsc, accessed August 15, 2023.

"Machine Olfaction," wikipedia, https://en.wikipedia.org/wiki/Machine_olfaction, accessed August 14, 2023.

"Machine Olfaction," Encyclopedia, Science News & Research Reviews, Academic Accelerator, https://academic-accelerator.com/encyclopedia/machine-olfaction, accessed August 14, 2023.

"Moral vs. Ethical: 3 Differences Between Ethics and Morals, MasterClass," October 23, 2022, https://www.masterclass.com/articles/moral-vs-ethical, accessed August 22, 2023.

OpenAI. (2023, June 14). What are the top 99 uses of Artificial Intelligence? [Response to user query]. In ChatGPT (Version 3.5) [Computer software]. OpenAI. Retrieved from [URL of this conversation]

OpenAI. (2023, June 14). "What are the top 100 concepts regarding artificial intelligence?"[Response to user query]. In ChatGPT (Version 3.5) [Computer software]. OpenAI. Retrieved from [URL of this conversation]

OpenAI. (2023, June 14). "Describe in detail how Siri works." [Response to user query]. In ChatGPT (Version 3.5) [Computer software]. OpenAI. Retrieved from [URL of this conversation]

"Rational Agent in AI: Intelligent Agents in Artificial Intelligence." Simplilearn, February 13, 2023, https://www.simplilearn.com/tutorials/artificial-intelligence-tutorial/rational-agent-in-ai#examples_of_rational_agents_in_ai, Accessed August 4, 2023.

"Remarks by President Biden on Standing up for Democracy," White House, November 3, 2022, https://www.whitehouse.gov/briefing-room/speeches-remarks/2022/11/03/remarks-by-president-biden-on-standing-up-for-democracy/, accessed August 28, 2023.

Sentient, "Sentient Definition & Meaning," Merriam-Webster, https://www.merriam-webster.com/dictionary/sentient, accessed August 14,2023.

"Six Dangers of AI! We Need to Pause it Now!" YouTube, https://youtu.be/M7xUj1QpGgI, Accessed August 14, 2023.

"Ten Things They Are Not Telling You About the New AI," https://youtu.be/qxbpTyeDZp0, accessed August 2, 2023.

"Transhumanism: 20 Ways It Will Change the World," Future Business Tech, YouTube, https://www.youtube.com/watch?v=qcsihbGnXgE, accessed June 7, 2023.

"Transhumanism: Merging Humans and Technology," June 25, 2023, Mirage News, https://www.miragenews.com/transhumanism-merging-humans-and-technology-1033779/,Accessed August 23, 2023.

United States Holocaust Memorial Museum, "Nazi Medical Experiments," Holocaust Encyclopedia, August 30, 2006, https://encyclopedia.ushmm.org/content/en/article/nazi-medical-experiments, accessed August 22, 2023.

Unveiling the Ten Stages of AI: What You Need To Know Now!, AI TechXplorer, https://youtu.be/AK5EwG62hx8, accessed July 31, 2023.

"U.S. Constitution | Constitution Annotated | Congress.gov | Library of Congress," https://constitution.congress.gov/constitution/preamble/, accessed August 26, 2023.

"What is a Cochlear Implant?" FDA, February 4, 2018, https://www.fda.gov/medical-devices/cochlear-implants/what-cochlear-implant#:~:text=A%20cochlear%20implant%20receives%20sound,experiences%20this%20as%20%22hearing%22, accessed August 21, 2023.

"Yes, Democrats Have Called Some Elections Illegitimate. "GOP Election Denialism Is Far Worse." CATO Institute, November 8, 2022, https://www.cato.org/commentary/yes-democrats-have-called-some-elections-illegitimate-gop-election-denialism-far-worse, accessed August 25, 2023.

Made in the USA
Monee, IL
31 August 2023

41907105R00115